"Attention all hipster pastors who want to reshape the church and world in your image—you do not want this book, but you really need this book. Pastor José Humphreys offers an authentic narrative not based on an unrealistic, romanticized view of urban church life (centered on coffee shops and organic grocery stores). This text provides a biblically and theologically robust vision of an embodied church that should provide a guidepost for the next generation of churches."

Soong-Chan Rah, Milton B. Engebretson Professor of Church Growth and Evangelism, North Park Theological Seminary, author of *The Next Evangelicalism* and *Prophetic Lament*

"It's simple, right? Show up. Stay put. See what God is doing. But it took pages of story-soaked sweat and tears, bleeding-edge exhortation, and street-savvy theological chops for the message to move from my brain to my body. This Puerto Rican pastor from East Harlem took me on a journey to a new way of seeing and being. Go get this amazing book. Get together with those you love (and those you wish you loved). And let's put this into practice!"

Paul Sparks, coauthor of *The New Parish*

"Do you want to know what the very good gospel looks like when lived out by the local church? Rev. José Humphreys writes down the vision and makes it plain. The result is a beautiful love letter to the church about how to be church in our browning, decolonizing world. Humphreys asks the two critical questions of all great pastors: 'What is the good news right here, right now?' and 'How does the body of Christ incarnate good news in gentrifying, shifting, gut-wrenching, awe-inspiring liminal space?' Rich with theological, sociological, and political insights, *Seeing Jesus in East Harlem* is every pastor's next must-read."

Lisa Sharon Harper, founder of Freedom Road LLC and author of *The Very Good Gospel*

"I believe we need a creative new generation of pastors and church planters today not just so we will have more churches but also so that we will have new kinds of churches—just as suited to our contexts as churches of the past were to theirs. *Seeing Jesus in East Harlem* is the story of one such church being birthed in the dynamic environment of East Harlem. You will meet a brilliant pastor, theologian, and writer José Humphreys, and you will be challenged to see your own congregation and context in a new light."

Brian D. McLaren, author of *The Great Spiritual Migration*

"José Humphreys's new book, *Seeing Jesus in East Harlem*, is an importa̶ ̶ ̶on-tribution to the church at this particular time in our nation's histor̶   ̶e continual growth of poor residents in our large cities, it is a̶ equipped with a contextual theology that speaks to the ne̶ and to the social realities in places like East Harlem ̶

Noel Castellanos, president of Christian Commu̶

"Prophetic urban pastor José Humphreys with a welcomed book on potential ways t̶   ̶xt. *Seeing Jesus in East Harlem* offers Pastor Hu̶   ̶an ministries. This critical and thoughtful book is al̶   ̶ing ministry beyond the context of the city. I highly recom̶   ̶one dealing with the challenges of germane ministry."

Samuel Cruz, associate professor of religion and society, Union Theological Seminary, senior pastor at Trinity Lutheran Church in Sunset Park, Brooklyn

"Jesus' teaching on the rich man in hell in Luke 16 haunts me, for it reminds me that comfort and privilege often blind me to the true nature of God's coming kingdom. Worse, I too often double down on my blindness by choosing to limit the theological voices I listen to. Wise is the one who searches for voices like José Humphreys and books like *Seeing Jesus in East Harlem*. This was a gift to my journey of following Jesus, and it will be to yours as well."

Daniel Hill, pastor, author of *White Awake*

"This is a splendid work! Inspiring, practical, and biblically wise, it asks astonishing questions about money, race, personality, the easy, hard, and messy parts of how we really live today, and what a church does that is really down in the ring with all of these. Humphreys is a grand storyteller in the biblical tradition—I laughed, smiled, and winced. This book will touch and guide anyone asking how biblical ideas connect to their lives."

Marcia Pally, professor of multilingual multicultural studies, New York University and Fordham University, author of *Commonwealth and Covenant*

"In this moment when gentrification seems inevitable and relocation is so trendy, the church desperately needs voices like José Humphreys's. Remaining has become a revolutionary act, and recognizing God amid marginalized communities is becoming a lost art. This book will empower you to do both, and it is a vital read for any believer longing to embody a counterculture neighborhood witness of presence and rootedness."

Dominique DuBois Gilliard, author of *Rethinking Incarceration*

"Sustainable embodied ministry requires practice and presence. Humphreys provides theological depth, pastoral wisdom, and practical tools that are deeply needed for communities seeking to be the church and not simply inhabiting a church building. This generation of church leaders needs to honestly ask if they are ready to reimagine how to live into a public and prophetic witness under the overwhelming realities of racial injustice, gentrification, and apathy toward the church. This story is one of honesty and hope."

Sandra Maria Van Opstal, pastor, activist, author of *The Next Worship*

"With *Seeing Jesus in East Harlem*, José proves himself a trustworthy guide, to faithful ministry at some of the crossroads of our culture's most important thoroughfares. These pages contain a beautiful and soaring vision, a call for our churches to 'cultivate ecologies of grace.' And because our guide has long planted his feet firmly in his context, it's a vision we can practically apply within our own."

David Swanson, pastor of New Community Covenant Church, Bronzeville, Chicago

"José Humphreys's *Seeing Jesus in East Harlem* is the best book on urban ministry in the twenty-first century. Calling Christ-centered leaders to stay rooted, relevant, and revolutionary in our age of global cities, *Seeing Jesus in East Harlem* should be required reading in our churches, colleges, and seminaries."

Peter Goodwin Heltzel, associate professor of theology, New York Theological Seminary

JOSÉ HUMPHREYS

SEEING JESUS IN EAST HARLEM

WHAT HAPPENS WHEN CHURCHES SHOW UP AND STAY PUT

IVP Books

An imprint of InterVarsity Press
Downers Grove, Illinois

InterVarsity Press
P.O. Box 1400, Downers Grove, IL 60515-1426
ivpress.com
email@ivpress.com

InterVarsity Press® is the book-publishing division of InterVarsity Christian Fellowship/USA®,
a movement of students and faculty active on campus at hundreds of universities,
colleges, and schools of nursing in the United States of America, and a member movement
of the International Fellowship of Evangelical Students. For information about local and
regional activities, visit intervarsity.org.

All Scripture quotations, unless otherwise indicated, are taken from The Holy Bible,
New International Version®, NIV®. Copyright © 1973, 1978, 1984, 2011 by Biblica, Inc.™
Used by permission of Zondervan. All rights reserved worldwide. www.zondervan.com.
The "NIV" and "New International Version" are trademarks registered in the United States
Patent and Trademark Office by Biblica, Inc.™

While any stories in this book are true, some names and identifying information may have
been changed to protect the privacy of individuals.

Cover design: David Fassett
Interior design: Jeanna Wiggins
Images: city apartment buildings: © NicolasMcComber / E+ / Getty Images
       grunge paper background: © enjoynz / iStock / Getty Images Plus

ISBN 978-0-8308-4149-3 (print)
ISBN 978-0-8308-7389-0 (digital)

Printed in the United States of America ∞

InterVarsity Press is committed to ecological stewardship and to the conservation of natural
resources in all our operations. This book was printed using sustainably sourced paper.

Library of Congress Cataloging-in-Publication Data

Names: Humphreys, José, 1972- author.
Title: Seeing Jesus in East Harlem : what happens when churches show up and
    stay put / José Humphreys.
Description: Downers Grove : InterVarsity Press, 2018. | Includes
    bibliographical references.
Identifiers: LCCN 2018022665 (print) | LCCN 2018031669 (ebook) | ISBN
    9780830873890 (eBook) | ISBN 9780830841493 (pbk. : alk. paper)
Subjects: LCSH: City churches. | City churches—New York (State)—New York.
Classification: LCC BV637 (ebook) | LCC BV637 .H86 2018 (print) | DDC
    253.09747/1—dc23
LC record available at https://lccn.loc.gov/2018022665

| P | 25 | 24 | 23 | 22 | 21 | 20 | 19 | 18 | 17 | 16 | 15 | 14 | 13 | 12 | 11 | 10 | 9 | 8 | 7 | 6 | 5 | 4 | 3 | 2 | 1 |
| Y | 37 | 36 | 35 | 34 | 33 | 32 | 31 | 30 | 29 | 28 | 27 | 26 | 25 | 24 | 23 | 22 | 21 | 20 | 19 | 18 |

This book is dedicated to my wife, Mayra,

my conversation partner on all things church and beyond.

Your perspective has been heaven's prism,

love's gentle light guiding me into more honest places.

Your courage and support have always lifted me,

and I've only become more

"strong at the broken places."

"Amores como el nuestro, se encuentran hoy ya menos."

Jerry Rivera

CONTENTS

INTRODUCTION

I LOVE THE LOCAL CHURCH, with all its hopes, dreams, and beautiful letdowns. Like a good dojo, it can be a rigorous space for learning how to love—a space for knowing God more through the practice of loving others well. And if truly open, the church can also be a space of experiment as we follow the Spirit's lead into new approaches to living, sharing, and showing signs of God's good news in our world.

Over the last eleven years or so I've had the privilege of leading a small, nimble, evangelical, ecumenical, multiethnic, transient church in East Harlem called Metro Hope. I believe that, like many other churches across cities, towns, and countries, we are a community leaving a beautiful imprint in our place. We have cultivated a family defined by God's work through our presence at one of the busiest intersections of the globe.

Life on the conveyor that is NYC can make the island feel more like a port of call than a destination. People come and go. Narratives converge (or collide) in a place where pace can prove antithetical to fostering deep community and transformation. I remember some time ago a pastor friend lamented over breakfast, "If the typical Manhattan person attends church about thirty Sundays per year for about one-and-a-half hours, an equivalent of forty-five hours, what kind of transformation can we truly expect?"

Like him, I often lament the institutional church's diminished role in society. Yet embedded in this challenge I envision an opportunity to reimagine our collective togetherness as part of God's larger plan for the way we live in the world—both huddled together and scattered forth after Sunday's benediction.

I've spent the last decade trying to figure out those forty-five hours in context. All the while I'm escaping the gravitational pull of the "good ol' days"—the times when church was a family's biggest priority, when church was for better or worse closer to the center of people's life rhythms. Now with the church largely decentered, I spend the majority of my time teaching others how to live as followers of Christ. I take a self-reflective, formative approach, anchoring people in practices and postures rooted in God's good news.

Through the life of Christ, the Scriptures demonstrate how discipleship is both intentional and incidental, even improvisational—through casual conversations over tables, walks in the community, being touched by suffering, and many other encounters beyond our Sunday venues, shaping us to become nimble and responsive to God's daily assignments.

Discipleship, viewed through a more generous gospel prism this way, can propel us into a wider-reaching, more vigorous faith. Meanwhile the practices of this faith can feel like the downward facing dog of the soul; while the posture looks easy enough, in practice it's difficult to sustain. But true faith dismantles illusions of false comforts and paper-thin theologies. The Spirit of God reminds us how adventures in growth are not without degrees of discomfort and tension. In truth, the Spirit's presence will draw us, even propel us, into paths less traveled—what the Bible describes as a narrow road.

In writing as a pastor, the "first disciple" of the local church, I have marked a path as a faithful practitioner in my context. This book should not be read as a one-stop, prepackaged what-to-do-for-ministry tool, but with an eye toward seeing and living more robustly in our calling to engage the crossroads of place, identity, race, diversity, and vocation (to name a few).

To create some markers for the journey, I've divided this book into three overarching themes. Each part defines postures and practices of Christian discipleship and ends with questions for further reflection. I outline these three themes in the following way.

Show Up—How are we individually and corporately responding to God's daily invitations and bringing our whole selves in truth and grace? This is our response to God's good news, rooted in an ever-broadening personal testimony (which is how we can reveal our true selves to the world). Our response is firmly based on the truth that God entered the world we know in body, as a first-century marginal Jew in Nazareth. We can draw clues about our own embodied presence in the world by way of Christ's.

Christ draws us by numerous invitations to serve from a deep sense of partnership with God and others. This will take courage, vulnerability, and knowledge of the times (discernment). The incarnation shows us that even though we are embedded in different realities through racial, theological, cultural, and economic stories, these stories don't have the final say about us as God's image bearers. To the degree that we as a church can individually and collectively practice being reflective about how we arrive and live into our stories, our neighbors, and our neighborhood, ecologies can be changed through God's shalom.

Staying Put—Are we richly dwelling with God and others while occupying and holding space together as church communities? Do we have the scriptural lenses, the contemplative resources, the emotional "bandwidth," and the conversational competencies to remain in crosscultural spaces of tension and transformation? Are we willing to slow down and learn from others? How must our thinking change in order to remain and bear fruit in the places we're called to?

Jesus invites us to dwell with him as we remain connected to others. God's love for us—for people—is vicarious this way. It works by engaging the messiness of this world and the beauty of relationships, and by recognizing that places as much as people can shape us as well.

In her engagement with the world, the church is challenged to continue to be of public consequence. This is a call not so much to remain relevant in the sense of being popular, but rather to be rooted and discerning the pulse of the times, responding to what is required of her in the moment. It's a contemplative way of inhabiting our zip codes.

Seeing—What proves to be the evidence of growth after we have shown up and stayed put in a place? One of the indicators of transformation is the way our questions about people, church, society, and even God begin to change. When we grow, we begin to see the image of God in more people than ever before. In seeing Jesus in our world, is our compassion reflex attuned to its hurt? How can some of the tools of the church's trade, our liturgy and sacraments, our way of interpreting culture, deeply engage the social realities and the suffering of our day?

Like the colorful murals found on brick walls in the *barrios* of East Harlem, I hope the stories I've curated at the intersections of a contextual discipleship can have universal yet contextual value anywhere. Each chapter in this book is expressed through personal narrative, helping readers reflect on a discipleship that takes personal salvation, public prophetic witness, and place into weighty consideration.

Here are some of the snapshots and scenarios:

- After a tense beginning, a group of extremely diverse church members agree on how to get a small group started in their neighborhood.

- A white person living into a call to be a part of a church of color faces the disorientation of choosing to stay.

- A church is called to stay as a local ally and to serve small businesses in a neighborhood that is gentrifying.

- In a city of hurry and expedience, a group of churches consider the worship service a parenthesis in the week where the rules of time are suspended and trauma isn't glossed over but enfolded in redemptive ways into God's greater narrative.

- Two white men live in intentional community with a Southern-born African American woman. They become family because of their many conversations over a kitchen island.

- A congregation is invited into a "fellowship of suffering" with the pastor and his wife after she is diagnosed with stage four lymphoma. It becomes a living moment, a story of showing up, staying put, and seeing the world of suffering differently.

My hope is this book will be considered an open source approach, a mustard seed contribution to the existing wisdom of many churches today and over the centuries—a continuing conversation for taking our formation in Christ further within our respective contexts, be they in city, town, or country.

Serious discipleship is about how God's Spirit can breathe healing and inspire new imagination into our immediate realities. A vision for deeper discipleship is then a necessity, and God's guest list will include all sorts of strange people who might not typically belong together. Together we can witness signs and snapshots of the kingdom if we learn to show up and stay put for the times we are called.

Indeed, it will be tough to stay put as we fumble around together, in a way reminiscent of the first church of Acts: steps behind God's Spirit, in tension with culture, perceived as never keeping up with the latest thinking. Moving together as a family will never happen quickly enough, packing for trips is stressful,

and agreeing on the best path forward can be tension ridden—
enough to keep us home settling for a movie and popcorn. But
who wants to stay home and spectate?

Here's my conviction about church ministry: whether big or
small, whether a church lasts with legacy or stays around for only
a season, we can't settle for being holding spaces for mere rituals.
We are called to be God's experiment in how people stay together
in a divided world. Now more than ever—whether churches are
in city, town, or country—we need churches that will dismantle
the walls of hostility that keep us apart, uncoiling people from
shame and hiding, allowing God's very good news to unfurl us all
into our full humanity as image bearers. I am grateful to play a
small part in such a grand and heavenly enterprise.

Today's world requires a deeper discipleship for the glory of
God and the good of our global family. Not just for our own sake,
but also for the sake of future generations who will eventually
show up for God's invitation.

We have plenty at stake.

PART 1

SHOW UP

1

EL TESTIMONIO
GO AND SHOW YOURSELF

If theology is contextual, it must certainly
be at root autobiographical.

JUNG YOUNG LEE

I **HEARD THE SOUND OF SIX GUNSHOTS** from my tiny
room in the housing projects.

A car screeched away via the East 10th Street roundabout,
with high-pitched screams quickly following. In my neighborhood, these sounds were a warning that bad news was on the
way. My neighbor Greg was shot during a drug deal gone wrong.
Friends near the scene had picked up Greg's bullet-ridden body,
driving him to a nearby hospital. But Greg would be DOA.

All in one flash of memory I remembered a lot about Greg. He
lived two floors directly above me. Greg would bully me some
days, but I remember the moment when he became a friend.
That one time when I rode my bike by the forbidden zone known

as East 8th Street, a bully knocked me off my bike and stole the seat. Greg found out, went to 8th Street, and "bullied the bully" into returning my seating paraphernalia. I realized then and there that hood justice could be a complex thing.

On this night, Greg would not be returning to his apartment two floors above; instead he had become the victim of yet another drug rivalry in the Lower East Side, Avenue D, the exiled corner of Manhattan island—a place where violence was commonplace.

LES in the 1980s was ripe with opportunities for bodily harm, and there was a well-founded paranoia for one's personal safety. This might mean walking with my security brigade (or as I affectionately called them, "my boys from the block") or making some on-the-spot decisions to walk four blocks west of my junior high school just to avoid certain crews. It was not out of the ordinary for us to be leery that even a simple pickup game at the basketball court could turn into a group fight. If we weren't on high alert for occasional dangers coming from neighborhood kids, we were just as afraid of having a run-in with the New York City Housing police.

Harm could also be hidden in the sporadic patches of grass, like that one time I fetched a sponge ball in the housing project patio. A hypodermic needle punctured my sneaker sole, running through it into my big toe. It was a terrifying moment when I believed I would get HIV/AIDS. Or at least that's what I feared, since no one was really sure how the disease was contracted. I remember being scared stiff on that bus ride to Bellevue Hospital, questioning whether my life was over at fifteen years old.

In the midst of this the church was always there, praying. Our little Latino Assemblies of God church was located four blocks southwest from our home, on the corner of 6th Street and Avenue C. Here *las hermanas* would pray almost every day of the week. Their prayers were every bit as gritty as our block. Intercession went out for the asthmatic kids in apartment 5C, kids who were probably suffering from the unknown effects of lead-based paint on housing project walls. And prayers were lifted for women like Doña Figueroa, who was to have her foot amputated because of diabetes, the result of living with poor medical care and limited healthy nutrition in the food swamp that was LES.

Then there were the spontaneous, real-time prayers that would take place on a crowded Avenue D. Like during that hot summer night walking back home from church when we watched Benito, a neighborhood addict, in the throes of another high. Mom would stop and pray. Others would just stop and watch Benito, "a junkie," doubling as street entertainment. The drug high would cause his body to contort, pulling off a gravity-defying stunt: his head drooping inches from the pavement—teasing, yet never quite touching it.

It was hard to name the veil of collective despair draped by NYC's summer smog in my neighborhood. The old church discerned this unnamed reality as spiritual warfare, a cosmic battle between angels and demons—spiritual darkness in high places. And I see that much as true: a living dis-integration, conditions conspiring to create a form of exile.

Many things contributed to this breakdown in our ecosystem known as the hood, including a failed education system, lack of investment in local infrastructure, and extreme poverty, with few resources to support people to cope, much less thrive.

My story, though, is more than just another glorified hood tale. On many days there were signs of grace and hope. These signs were embodied in people like Ms. Brown, the head of the tenants' association. Ms. Brown planted a garden that would grow in the midst of NYCHA's signature red brick. She would also cuss us out with great zeal—especially if her heirloom tomatoes became casualties of our stickball games.

Spontaneous block parties and barbecues reminded us that even gated project patios were our back yard. With no green space, or "no trespassing," there would be no problem. We would get creative with space in our neighborhood and arrange life on public places, namely our sidewalks. Community became a concrete form of resistance. One of the ways this was facilitated was through the neighborhood liturgists otherwise known as DJs. They would show up with their turntables and others with cardboard boxes, creating a party-in-a-box atmosphere. People were ready to "battle"—to dance and celebrate good music with superior dance skills.

In the air there was this sense of acceptance of one another in sharing a place together. People on the block tolerated and even loved this lanky Latino church boy. Everyone looked out for each other's children, and Mami had an open fridge policy for all my friends.

To ensure our continual safety, no stranger could enter the housing project unless Mr. Rodriguez from the first floor would approve it and Mr. Smith from the tenants association would second it.

Ours was a resilient community with God's image all over it. There were divine signs and snapshots of beauty. It was quite reminiscent of James Baldwin's Harlem experience when he wrote, "Perhaps we were, all of us—pimps, whores, racketeers, church members, and children—bound together by the nature of our oppression, the specific and peculiar complex of risks we had to run; if so within these limits we sometimes achieved with each other a freedom that was close to love."

Today, when I visit with my mom and dad, they refuse to leave LES. Whenever I attempt to convince Mami to move to Puerto Rico, she becomes adamant, saying, "No. No. *Manhattan es mi isla.*"

Presently Mami's neighborhood is a mostly gentrified, fancy restaurant–laden, university-inhabited neighborhood. The poverty and drug activity is now hemmed farther east, mostly into one avenue, while boutiques and trendy bars have replaced bodegas and barbershops.

Gentrification, they say, has good intentions, on paper at least. But there are unintended consequences that come with such so-called development. If neighborhoods continue to be "discovered" in a form unchecked, without nuances in neighborhood policy, gentrification simply creates a new form of a hipster-ghetto, hidden in trendiness, cut off from a history that once was. One will simply find an alternate numbness in the same hood. The elite become less whole when disconnected from the neighbor who is unable to make rent next door. Unjust transactions happen when systems profit from someone's inability to stay in a place.

Historically, certain political groups within our country have attached upward mobility to morality. If a person isn't somehow able to climb out of poverty, they must be too lazy to scale the ladder. I noticed that when I found a few more rungs on this elusive ladder, the world began to see me just a little bit more. The more visible someone becomes, somehow, the less "ghetto" they are. To live what is deemed a "respectable" middle-class existence can somewhat make one feel removed from one's beginnings—but not totally.

As migrants from Puerto Rico in the 1950s, my parents worked hard to see their children educated to make an impact in our world. My parents always grounded us in care for our neighbors as an extension of a feet-to-the-ground kind of faith, always reminding us in one way or another how relative privilege can easily become a brittle platform the moment we see ourselves as better or different from others.

Most importantly, my parents left me a great inheritance through *Cristo, mi salvador personal*, who I met at the storefront Pentecostal church on 6th Street. *Cristo* was a healer and teacher, one who walked the streets of the cities, towns, and countries, looking for those who are down and out. *Cristo* continues to make everyday invitations to show up, to stay with me, to help me see the world differently.

Being a follower for most of my life now, I find that this cosmic Christ is located in many, many more places than I could've imagined. One sign of this personal formation is an ever-expanding testimony of how Christ's love pursues me even through the personal ruptures of my being, undeterred by the real-time messiness of my given realities.

I find that when Christ shows up, our stories become integrated into the life of Christ himself. In the mutuality of our lives, Christ shows up in both places of wholeness and places of unraveling, and we see his grace and mercy everywhere. Christ repairs the breaches so our personal and societal narratives become complete. He frames our stories so that we show up infused with meaning, dressed to life's party as our redeemed selves.

Knowing what these breaches look like—what I have come to know as sin—has been vital for an ever-growing testimony. It's the story of me, the story of us, but it was also the story of Adam and Eve in a garden. Our stories are just some of billions of minute marks on the human storyboard, billions of small narratives among the many more that continue to unfold over time. Our human family as a whole holds a history of wounds and trauma that come from broken exchanges between people, rooted in the breakdowns caused by sin in our world. Wounded people, wounded systems, wounding others over time and place.

For each tear in the fabric of God's intended wholeness, there is, or can be, a testimony of a gospel that repairs those breaches, with grace working specifically and uniquely at each place. But to construct a more whole testimony is to realize how (1) sin causes breakdowns that are relational and (2) Christ's redeeming embrace invites us to show ourselves in the world as image bearers, with our testimonies as a holy work.

SIN IN OUR STORY: AN ECOLOGICAL BREAKDOWN

Testifying about Christ's goodness often means locating the ruptures in life, the breakdowns caused by sin, where Christ meets us. When I teach about the breakdowns that come from sin, there is rarely an apathetic response in the church pews. For some it is a top-ten, favored Christian topic, and for others . . . not so much.

A handmade knit scarf is an unlikely but best picture by far for describing sin as a breakdown in relationships. When Abuelita knits your six-year-old son a scarf, it's a labor of love that, regardless of the season, he is obligated to wear with pride. But what happens when your little Juancito pulls the loose thread? Abuelita's knitted labor of love becomes unraveled. The beauty, character, and integrity of what was to be worn is now tattered.

Abuelita's knit scarf is one of many ways to look at the effects of what we call sin. Cornelius Plantinga describes sin as an "unraveling of shalom." If shalom is the quality of wholeness, harmony, and flourishing in God's creation, sin is a violation of it.

Genesis tells the story of God's good creation. It also tells the story of humanity's desperate grasping after forbidden fruit, and the hiding that happened as a result of taking more than what God intended. Resultantly, the first man and the first woman would no longer see each other the same way. Somehow the image of God was obscured in their viewing of each other. Bodies became objects of shame; the being-ness of showing up naked and unashamed was lost.

In the unraveling of human relationship with God, the whole creation felt its effects. Adam and Eve not only experienced a breakdown with God but compromised the conditions for relational flourishing through their sin, because flourishing happens in connection to God *through* people, including through their work. God provides people with work as one means of communicating God's own love to the world.

Relational breakdowns can happen when a person's desires are misappropriated or disordered. Grasping for more than what God has for us has become a continual sickness of the soul and our world. You can trace these breakdowns through the Old Testament, which makes any episode of *Game of Thrones* look like an episode of *Full House*.

In her book *The Very Good Gospel*, Lisa Sharon Harper sums it up well:

> In the Hebrew conception of the world, all of creation is connected. The well-being of the whole depends on the well-being of each individual part. The Hebrew conception of goodness was different than the Greeks'. The Greeks located perfection within the object itself. A thing or a person strove toward perfection. But the Hebrews understood goodness to be located between things. As a result the original hearers would have understood *tov* [the Hebrew word

for good] to refer to the ties of relationships between things in creation.

Since the garden, people have been grasping for a fullness or harmony between things that, to date, has evaded our best efforts through systems such as education, governments, the courts, or even technological advancements. While human ingenuity is a sign of God's image, we've seen many of these advancements and systems fall short and become signs toward a witness of a world deeply divided.

It wasn't just my theological training that provided me clarity about how these breakdowns unfold in the world, but my social work education, through a theory called the Ecological Perspective, which borrows from elements of biology (and, one could say, creation). It's helpful for seeing how our world is interconnected through different systems. Whenever we speak of things unraveling, it's due to "dysfunctional transactions between people and their physical and social environments."

Our world consists of micro systems such as individuals, families, and religious systems. These micro systems are connected to larger systems like schools and communities, and macro systems like economies and governments. And when any of these systems break down, it can cause a pervasive ripple, leading to breakdowns in the health of other systems. We call this the classic ripple effect.

Evidence of a disrupted ecology can be found in so much of our everyday twenty-first-century world, demonstrated in the life of our varying systems from institutions to families and individuals. The effects are far reaching, even passed down from one generation to the next.

Breakdowns exist in relationship to our bodies through highly stressful environments. This is demonstrated in epigenetics, a field that researches how a person's genes can be altered by trauma, stress, and even poor diet. These can actually create constitutional changes in genes passed down to younger generations.

An interview in *Psychology Today* describes how PTSD from Holocaust survivors was transmitted to younger generations, both through secondary trauma (listening to the stories of their traumatized parents) and through altered genetics. Stress hormones such as cortisol can have significant effects on a person's physiology, leading to constitutional changes in DNA. In a related interview Dr. Rachel Yehuda discusses how the children of certain Holocaust survivors were "several times more likely to develop post-traumatic stress disorder, if they were exposed to a traumatic event."

These physiological stresses due to larger systems and forces (Hitler's government) demonstrate the collateral consequences of sin and how these consequences can be transmitted from one generation to the next. Similar collateral consequences can be found in neighborhoods with extreme poverty or in the breakdown of families due to overpolicing and a punitive prison culture—leading to trauma passed down across space and time.

Indeed there are a multiplicity of breakdowns in both our personhood and our society. More than ever we need to recover a more robust gospel that engages this expanse. Paul said, "Where sin increased, grace increased all the more" (Romans 5:20). The collision between God's good news and our places of unraveling becomes the basis of our testimony.

In light of this, could it be that our understanding of the gospel needs to be redeemed? For as many breakdowns that exist, Christ redeems, repairs, and continues redeeming through a multiplicity of signs and wonders, pointing us to a place of righteousness, justice, peace, and joy—heaven.

In the Scriptures, each of Christ's miracles pointed to a whole gospel for the whole world, yet was localized for particular needs. That's what made Jesus' ministry holistic, restorative, and integrative: each sign and wonder tethered people back to God, with those who experienced miracles becoming a sign to others of God's wondrous work.

Christ's miracles were each distinct in recognizing the multiple ways that the tears in the fabric of shalom can label people, separate them, or keep them apart. From freeing a demon-possessed man and sending him back home to testify, to healing skin diseases that made exiles of people, Jesus' works addressed the issues that would cause people to hide or be outcast.

In Luke 17:11-19, Jesus demonstrated this restorative and integrating approach on the road to Jerusalem. Ten lepers had come running to him for healing. Jesus told them, "Go, show yourselves to the priests." And as they went forth in faith they were healed. To show oneself to a priest was to receive a blessing of integration back into the social fabric, a place among the people.

Of the ten lepers, one would return to Jesus with gratitude, recognizing from where his true restoration and insertion into the life of the world came. The one who returned in gratitude— the Samaritan—was the only one of the ten who showed himself to Jesus, the true high priest. Together, like this Samaritan, we Gentiles today continually show ourselves to Jesus and others in gratitude, singing the old gospel song for the world to hear: "Look what the Lord has done. He healed my body, he touched my mind. He saved me, just in time." We've been enjoined into God's good plans.

We participate in the practice of fellowship, we create and hold spaces where we can show ourselves as an exercise of faith, as a measurement of maturity. Through our collective vulnerability in Christ, others can hear this message and become uncoiled from their own exile and hiding.

TESTIMONIO: AN INTEGRATING PRACTICE

In my work as a church pastor, if I had been simply focused on church sustainability and mega-growth, I would've missed what signs and wonders could look like in our context. But when one is measuring success at the breakdowns, the idea is not just creating permanent structures but locating the fruit that will last in people. In 2 Corinthians 3:2 Paul reminds us that the greatest testimonies are not made of brick and mortar but people's lives for the world to see.

Recognizing the practice of testimony as a mark for both personal and communal growth is vital. Our church has only recently begun to recover this practice from the old Pentecostal church as a form of shaping memories of God's goodness and a way of honoring God's activity in the simplest and most profound of ways. Sunday services are not always set up for this kind of intimacy. Even small groups at times can become more of a heady exercise than not. But our ongoing testimonies carry a real-time story about God working in the here and now. As theologian Eldin Villafane writes, *testimonio* is one way of locating the Spirit's activity through the church in the world.

Church gatherings have been and can still be spaces where testimonies can break down educational and class barriers, where even the woman with the third grade education can stand up in the authority of God, naming God's miracle at the breaches. I once heard a woman proclaiming how her son had been a drug addict, but now was liberated from heroin. He encountered the power of the Spirit in church and became instantaneously free from his addiction. No symptoms. No signs of withdrawal. No rehab. God's liberating gospel bringing forth an instantaneous mending.

Take it from this skeptic—my eyes have seen this and are challenged again and again. *El evangelio* (the gospel) brings in a new announcement of lives now under the jurisdiction of Jesus. We stand today with the many *hermanas* in the church who were planting the cross, a tree, in the ground of grace. They were claiming God's authority as they described the work of *Cristo* in their own language— *Cristo* who was working within their story in their time and place.

Testimonios curate momentary snapshots of a more enduring wholeness to come, of the healing envisioned in the book of

Revelation where the exiled apocalyptic pastor wrote, "The river of the water of life . . . [flowed] down the middle of the great street of the city. On each side of the river stood the tree of life, bearing twelve crops of fruit, yielding its fruit every month. And the leaves of the tree are for the healing of the nations." The great promise of heaven is that God will take the distinct particular pains of each nation and bring healing. Each story will be included. No one's pain will be minimized or classify him or her unworthy. People's primordial wounds will be healed through the grace of the Ancient of Days.

But for now, all we have are our testimonies pointing to God's activities. The more we see how sin contextualizes itself in our lives and takes root in the life of society, the more we can become discerning in our dealings at these breakdowns. This is why we need to train our people to practice testimony, to recount what God is doing in their lives across multiple facets of life. To detect God's loving presence at the breakdowns is the basis for the practice of testimony.

As I have shown up with others, others have shown up with me. Together we've witnessed God's work in several forms that will expand through the following chapters. We need the Spirit's power for a sustained engagement that will allow us to see God's work again and again in real time. We can practice a discipleship that earnestly engages the breaches, testifying to how God has rebuilt our disconnections.

Jesus' redeeming love draws us to God and turns us outward to the world with the face of the church. The church then proclaims a gospel that addresses both personal and systemic unraveling. If not robust in this manner, our gospel will do a disservice to discipleship, encouraging an overly personalized testimony, which inevitably turns people inward.

To recover a full gospel is to see Christ in more places than ever, tethering the breakdowns in self and the world, locating God's web of grace that holds us and heals us, encouraging us to show ourselves again and again.

REFLECTION QUESTIONS

1. Describe your first encounter with faith and Christ. If raised in the faith, what beauty did you find in your own faith narrative growing up?

2. What was your understanding of the gospel when you first received it?

3. How has your understanding of Christ, the gospel, and the work of the church expanded over time? Where do you see places of greater awareness and expansion?

4. What is your own story of personal breakdown?

5. What are the ruptures or breakdowns in your neighborhood or city?

6. How is your understanding of the gospel connected to this breakdown?

7. What are the signs that God is at work in the breakdowns?

8. How have your eyes continued to open and your testimony continued to develop?

2

THE "HERE I AMS" OF LIFE

CALLING AND HOLY DISORIENTATION

What if this darkness is not the darkness of
the tomb, but the darkness of the womb?

VALARIE KAUR, SIKH ACTIVIST

NEIL GOLDBERG IS A NATIVE NEW YORKER and a media artist whose work has been exhibited in places like the Museum of the City of New York, the Guggenheim, and the MoMa. Goldberg's art has a distinct way of taking the most mundane everyday moments in New York City and somehow turning them into a conversation piece.

My wife and I caught one of his exhibits in 2012. The exhibit was every bit as quirky as it was fascinating. From a series of videos that zoomed in on New Yorkers' facial expressions as they made lunch decisions at a salad bar, to a facial montage focusing

on the moment shop owners lift the front gate screens up to open for business in the morning, Goldberg records everyday moments of people simply showing up to life.

Of all the works we witnessed, our favorite was called *Surfacing*, a silent video series. Goldberg focused on people's facial expressions the moment they emerged from the subway station. As consummate people watchers, we were tickled. The expressions were as diverse as the people who surfaced. There was a human quality about that moment of arrival; it communicated a range of feelings from vulnerability to surety to looking lost and disoriented—this was the power of the art.

One African American woman rises up, grimacing, out of breath from her walk up the stairs. But a few steps beyond the top of the landing, her eyes are confidently fixed on where she is going. There is a Latino man looking casual as he comes up, a NY Yankee cap giving him that extra swagger for the journey.

An older woman surfaces looking somewhat lost; she mumbles something under her breath as she peruses the street signs, perhaps repeating the name of her intended destination. A middle-aged Caucasian man with a receding hairline surfaces, chewing gum, looking intensely into the bustling city. If the look could speak, it would say, "I may have been here before. But I'm still finding my way."

Goldberg says, "The moment of emerging from the subway is always sort of like waking up . . . like coming back into your life."

A connoisseur of art I am not, but in my pastoral role I have been trained to make divine connections with most everything. Or at least I've been accused of doing so. I connected deeply with this visual experience of emergence—how people show up to the daily "here I ams" of life. For the follower of Christ, responding daily to God's invitations means life is full of redemptive possibilities, brimming with heavenly purpose.

From the earliest involuntary invitation out of our mother's womb, we emerge, we breach, we breathe our first breath, followed by our first cry, letting the world know, "here I am." We will then grow through life receiving many more invitations to "surface," or participate in the life of the world.

For my wife, Mayra, and me, one of the most formative "here I am" moments came when starting a diverse church community in East Harlem. For us it was getting to join Jesus in the sacred maternity ward, birthing a dream where a church could seek God's racial justice and spiritual renewal in the span of a few square blocks. All the while we held deep within us Dr. King's lament about how 11 a.m. on a Sunday morning is the most segregated hour in America.

Most sociologists would agree that people unite mostly around commonalities such as race, class, and common ways of looking at faith tradition. We had no idea how societal forces would push back when we challenged these daunting trends. To challenge any one of those categories is disorienting. To challenge more of those categories—at the same time—is a form of naiveté, a recipe for some serious disorientation.

But through our many mistakes and experiences, we have become navigators of some complex ministry terrain in a pluralistic world. We have found that Christian formation can thrive through sustained practices of healthy conversation, working through emotional landscapes of discomfort and disorientation and continual repentance.

While we have found this work to be much more aspirational than actual, as our church is far from this ideal place, we can confidently attest to witnessing snapshots and moments of the kingdom in our efforts together. But it didn't come without disorienting invitations and conversations, all incidental material for our own growth. I recognized I was not alone in responding to Christ's invitation. The biblical narratives of the apostle Peter grounded us, especially in the beginning stages, as we were sent forward with a group of twelve.

PRACTICE INVITATION: DISORIENTING CONVERSATIONS

I find that a calling in the Christian life can bring us through periods of great joy and great disorientation, where we receive Christ's invitation only to realize how short we fall of its demands. The Scriptures also show us how we're in good company with a fellowship of the disoriented.

In Luke 5 Peter finds himself in a boat with a miraculous catch of fish. This moment had come after some conversation—some back and forth with Jesus (who was unrecognized at the time) about throwing the net back into the water at his behest. Peter and his crew had fished all night without result, so the invitation to go fishing again would naturally seem counterintuitive. But those who follow Christ often find the call comes this way—we may have attempted ministry in our own strength, yet are encouraged to try again. Why? Because like Peter, when we can respond with "only because you say so," our openness may become the penultimate material for miracles to take place.

Only after Peter and his companions caught the miraculous catch of fish—to the point the nets were almost breaking—did he realize who this man on the boat was. In a disoriented fit Peter exclaimed, "Go away from me, Lord; I am a sinful man!" (Luke 5:8). Peter realized who Jesus was and realized his own exile and separation from God's intended wholeness for him. Jesus' response, I find, is a cure to any person who thinks God has some extreme fixation with sin, some "gotcha" attitude, as some would teach. Jesus simply responded, "Come, follow me, and I will send you out to fish for people."

What a beautiful invitation! Christ's invitation would put in proper perspective Peter's fragmentation—humanity's fragmentation—in light of a Christ who would call him into a new allegiance, a new kingdom. Just show up! And through the journey "I will send you . . ."

Only when this grace-filled invitation imprints on our hearts—this world-changing, mind-boggling, and reorienting invitation—are we changed. For us to realize our own insufficiency, no matter how gifted we think we are, is a healthy form of engagement. God calls us to something greater than ourselves, so a healthy disorientation—not knowing how we're going to do this, or even an "I don't exactly know where this is going"—is the call of faith for those following Rabbi Jesus in wonder and amazement.

Jesus not only enters our boat, our space, offering a life-changing invitation, but he also offers his presence in continuing conversation. Jesus and Peter would have many conversations about God's work in the world that would prove disorienting and formative to Peter. These invitations would define Peter, and he would seem to get it wrong more than right.

It was this story, in some ways, that gave Mayra and me a foundation for inviting others to show up into this continuing conversation we call faith.

The church was the fruit of many, many conversations. The moment Jesus stepped into our own work space we envisioned starting a multiethnic, multicultural church with a more whole and integrated view of Jesus and the gospel. We yearned for a church that would hold together both personal and public dimensions of faith and that would be shaped by an ecumenical ethos. Yes, it was absolutely naive. But somehow in our showing up we continued to hold on to the "confidence in what we hope for and assurance about what we do not see" (Hebrews 11:1).

In 2007, in response to the call, we began a group in the American Bible Society called Conversations with God and One Another. Conversations would facilitate a "sacred space." It was also a quirky space where white, black, Asian, and Latino/a folks showed up, as well as some Pentecostal-evangelicals, a couple of agnostics, a couple of Christian anarchists, and a Muslim. We sounded like the beginning of a good joke you tell at a bar over a shot of bourbon.

Some of us were questioning faith—putting these questions out in public for the first time. Our questions were not deep existential questions about the meaning of life or suffering. The questions were more ecclesial and relational in nature, about broken fellowship and disappointments with the church. We had an idea that divisions existed in the larger church in general. But we didn't know why the church remained so largely segregated across race and class boundaries—even in NYC, a supposedly progressive town. Even church planting movements still carry the tendency to work around the homogenous unit principle, trying to gather like-minded upper-class professionals in up-and-coming neighborhood settings. The movements in many ways can perpetuate the racial and class divides consistent with the larger divides in our country.

Practicing conversations became a redemptive experience: a healing space for spiritual friendships among the most unlikely, a safe space where people could paint conversational strokes on parts of the canvas off limits in other faith circles. Conversations in a diverse context are a formative affair, as we witnessed. Creating invitations for others—being merely exposed to diverse people in facilitated conversation—led to changes in people's attitudes toward one another.

In conversations the miracles were subtle yet undeniable. One common refrain heard after each experience was, "The space is a breath of fresh air." The Spirit began to provide oxygen to those fatigued by a gospel story too narrow for a complex and ever-changing world. And through our time together conditions were created for people to grow into a more integrated faith.

In cultivating artful conversation Mayra and I were more facilitators than teachers. We had faith that God's generous Spirit was flowing like streams through each person, drawing them to share what was needed for the moment. We arrived with pointed questions about the role of faith and society, and people shared from their life intersections with great passion.

Like a surgeon in pre-op, Mayra prayerfully prepared people to enter into the space by setting the groundwork through words of welcome and letting people know what to expect. I took the time to think of Scripture texts that could be contextualized. We laid down the necessary antecedents in an attempt to prepare people not for just sensitive subject matter but for opinions that could be distinctively different from their own.

One of Mayra's common refrains was, "If you're going to be a part of a diverse community, be prepared to be pissed off." For the most part early on people were simply enthralled with what the space represented: an infusion of faith, imaginations stirred around what church could actually be like.

For some people, an angry hunter God became more of a loving pursuer. For others it was the chance to be introduced (or re-introduced) to a new Christ. Some carried old wounds and trauma from spiritual abuse in the hands of the church. Others sought a deeper integration between a personal and public faith. We broached topics like politics, race, church life, and even sexuality.

False or narrow God concepts were not the only thing expanded. People's hearts expanded to embrace personal stories they could deeply resonate with. Each story became part of all who had the privilege of hearing, because people were sharing so vulnerably.

One young Latina from Colombia named Angelly shared about a certain policy called the Dream Act, which was personally important to her. The Dream Act would give her and others like her an opportunity to attend college. Angelly arrived in this country with her family at the age of three. Because she was undocumented, it somehow didn't matter that she was educated and raised in this country. Or that she was as culturally American as anyone else. Angelly was in constant fear of deportation, and yet our forum allowed her to share these fears with the group and even take them public.

Tom, who was a sixty-seven-year-old Irish Jesuit Catholic from Massachusetts, was struck at the heart when he heard Angelly's testimony. He had lived in this country his whole life yet never felt such compassion and hurt for someone undocumented. Tom had been working with Latino/as for fifteen years in the South Bronx, but somehow the sacred proximity provided by Conversations allowed him an instant connection with suffering in a more nuanced way. He now became vigilant about a certain plight he might have overlooked in the past. Not because he became politically informed, but because he heard Angie's story and heard her fears while in close relationship with her.

Derek and JP were progressive Christians who were squatting in an abandoned building in Brooklyn. Derek and JP would take in the homeless and provide them with shelter and a form of case management. Derek spent a fair amount of time with our group. We found him to be truly dedicated to the teachings of Christ in ways that were radical. His approach to the Scriptures disoriented some in our group because he would take the red letters of Scripture seriously, and he would also consistently call into question his own white privilege. While many were tempted to reduce the Beatitudes to hyperbole, here was someone who was living then out in ways that were impacting us all.

Sara was of mixed heritage, both white and Peruvian. She was at the intersection of Islam and Christianity, with each of her parents holding to their faiths. Sara was gentle and grounded. She was a breath of fresh air. Hers was the honest struggle that comes with Islam—acknowledging Christ as Lord. Yet the space was able to hold her too. Sara's openness to us in the midst of her questions was awesome. Time and time again I felt it was a privilege that she would hang out with evangelicals.

Patty was a young Puerto Rican who identified as spiritual but not religious, yet was drawn to the questions. We had folks like Ana, Joed, and Joey from the Latino/a church, who were looking for a more integrated gospel. Some wounded, some anxious from years of guilt-ridden, performance-based Christianity. They were looking for Christ outside of the model of church ministry. One underlying question from our time together was, "How can one ever replace the sort of tight-knit community of a first-generation Pentecostal church experience?"

Charles was one of our community anchors. He was African American and "bapticostal"; I guess that's a blend between Baptist and Pentecostal. Charles was from great ministry stock. His father pastored in Maryland for over thirty years. Charles brought the "boom" into preaching, and he was grounded in the black tradition of the church. As someone who was raised as an only child he gave Mayra and me hope through our neuroticism as parents—hope that our only child could become well-adjusted like him one day.

I was grateful that Charles stuck around even when I allowed dominant culture values to swing the pendulum in our worship to being more white. One time when I asked Charles how we could integrate more of his experience, Charles said, "Just get a piano, doc." Charles's comment cannot be minimized to a matter about worship style preference. Traditional African American worship hearkens back to churches as havens of black affirmation and resistance to a narrative that made black lives second rate and marginal at best.

Frank, a sculptor who was highly influenced by the emergent movement, had a passion for reaching artists in NYC. He had been living in East Harlem for the previous year. He saw some promise and potential in our little church experiment. Frank also complained to me about how East Harlem somehow offended his aesthetic sensibilities. He saw rundown buildings, empty business spaces, and not much activity on his block. He said that East Harlem felt "drab and without character."

I said, "Don't worry, gentrification will cure that. We'll be looking like Portland, Oregon, in no time."

Our group was at the intersections of offending and being offended. And frankly, it simply demonstrated a truth we know well. Deep down inside we all have the potential to be divisive and limited in our perspectives, and this potential only becomes magnified in diversity. Maybe Reinhold Niebuhr was onto something when he described how groups tend to be more sinful than individuals.

If Babel's story is a case study about homogeneity, Pentecost shows us that diversity can be unnatural unless the Spirit helps us. We were all disoriented in some ways. Perhaps it would've been easier to wrestle with these questions with others we shared more in common with. But we were willing to expand the bandwidth of our collective vulnerability . . . to a point.

Our group mustered enough momentum and went away to a retreat at Spruce Lake, a historically Methodist retreat center. The intent was to cast vision about a new church we were starting in Manhattan. Every pastor knows the potential power of a retreat. Hay rides, s'mores by the fire, and an openness and clarity one could only receive away from the city hustle.

An energy and grace was present and palpable. People were engaging in intimate conversations about faith. There was an openness to learn from one another. It was fun with everyone enjoying the sincerity of one another's company. I really thought it was a snapshot of what heaven would be like.

All was very good until that conversation on the last day. It was a conversation some of us were ready for, but most of us were not. Mayra and I had prepared a discussion based on a book called *They Love Jesus but Not the Church,* by Dan Kimball. It had a list of topics about why people were turned off to the church. These turnoffs ranged from politics to sexuality, and the book was about experiences with (white) millennials.

Things went well as we moved from politics through different matters. But something happened when sexuality came up. The goodwill that had been brought together seemed to be vacuumed out of the room. Some committed followers of Christ were affirming of same-sex relationships, and others were not. And I was the facilitator trying to moderate the conversation. Those who were affirming cried out, "How could I bring my gay friends here?" while others didn't believe that Christians could even be gay.

We all left the retreat divided as a result. Meanwhile, Mayra and I left for Miami that week wondering if we would still have a core group intact upon returning. A few days at the beach away from ministry did us good. Looking back at the beginning of our church plant, every setback felt fatal.

Miraculously, when we returned, everyone attended the next gathering. We found that people had bonded too much with one another to just abandon the group. Even in the midst of vehement disagreement, love could not be denied. It was the

Spirit's grace that held our small gathering together. Every time the adhesive that bonded the group together somehow dulled, the Spirit's unity would prevail.

Safety for us was not so much the abatement of fear, but the honoring of each person's story as sacred and worth sharing. The reason everyone stood together is because of their willingness to experience some degree of vulnerability and discomfort, and because of their willingness to endure the disorientation of difference, yet remain held in community.

These are snapshots of togetherness. I've never made a monument of this moment because we realized that it was what it was supposed to be: a moment in time in the church plant—a space that could not be intentionally duplicated. I still see the potential of such spaces, and how a conversant church can be a place for rigorous engagement—where we practice a form of contortion, stretching into a more nimble faith that can help us engage a complex world more generously.

Every individual and every institution has a starting point for these discussions. One denomination's starting point will be different from another's. Each context will bring its own complexities, limitations, and possibilities. That's without even factoring in theological and doctrinal tensions.

Choosing to stay, and stay committed, in a church family and denominational family is a calling, I believe. Ultimately it is a calling for people to show up in these tensions and work through narratives, values, and cultural moments.

But none of this can be sustained without a continual posture of openness and repentance. To discern the gifts we are to receive from people for the limited amount of time we're together requires an open heart.

How is our time together in prayer and connection with God and one another making us more humble? Because of the grace given to us, it behooves the church to foster spaces where people can "get it wrong"—a place where we can potentially offend and be offended. There's a time to interrogate language, and there's a time to enter into the messy process of relationship, ready to receive and extend grace. Ideally, is not the church where such radical grace is extended? We're then challenged to aspire to church cultures where this form of disorientation can be taken into account toward a more radical inclusiveness.

From its inception, this has been the trajectory of the church in its "groan zones" of disorientation and its subsequent growth. For that reason I bring us back to the life of Peter—who "fumbled" forward again in another story—grounding us in the truth that sacred trajectories are riddled with error.

ENCOUNTER AND REPENTANCE: REPENTANCE AS ULTIMATE VULNERABILITY

Divine encounters, whether with God or God's children, can leave us feeling vulnerable. When we try our best to be united rather than uniform, we may find that our world is a lot more divided than we suspected. Showing up together and uniting

around our differences takes time and energy, while unconscious fear prevents us from loving others more radically.

In these spaces we can encounter God at the breaches of our
phobias, submitting to the truth that our feeble attempts at
mending the world need to fall under Christ's jurisdiction.
Otherwise we become complicit in separating and creating
further divisions in our world. We can ignore those who matter
to God because of our inability to show up and cross bridges.

If you're ever feeling that you continually fall short in this
manner, then, like me, make the apostle Peter your go-to guy for
setting a precedent for how to reject others. You'll see someone
who stumbled around trying to get it right with people, especially around diversity. We're blessed to have this window into
the life of Peter and his public foibles.

Peter, one of the first apostles, faced continuing disorientation
in church mission following the work of the Holy Spirit. Paul's
letter to the Galatians recounts a time Peter was sharing a meal
with some Gentiles. A modern storyline could read, "Why are all
the Gentiles sitting together in the cafeteria?"

Peter, upon seeing some Judaizers walk in, found himself in a
self-conscious moment. Going by Jewish memory and law, he
reacted by moving to another table.

Paul, who narrates this event in Scripture, happened to be
sitting nearby. Paul may have understood well the pressures
Peter was feeling. After all, Paul was a devout practicing Jew as
well, a self-proclaimed Pharisee of Pharisees.

While Paul was watching Peter play musical tables, shuffling to recline somewhere else, he knew Peter was not "acting in line with the truth of the gospel" (Galatians 2:14).

Like Peter, at one time or another we might find ourselves switching tables. Not taking a stand for others who God loves fiercely. We find ourselves favoring those who are "in."

Peter is a reminder that the knowledge of God's embracing love does not necessarily lead to the practice of it. Paul's challenge to Peter was not a simplistic moral argument over right and wrong, not in doctrinal appeals nor in proof texting, but in his posture and location in God's great story of embracing, grafting, integrating love.

Are our actions in line with the truth of the gospel?

It is a question rooted in Peter's proximity to Gentile believers who were once strangers to God's promise. Peter's initial table-hopping reaction only served to shrink the table that was to be more inclusive of more of God's children.

We who are in this work of integration and embrace, reconciling people back to God and one another, can be thankful for these key moments in Peter's life. In the midst of his public foibles, Peter was not afraid to come back and say "here I am" again and again. Yet chances are that while many of us can relate to Peter on some level, we who are reading the text are most likely Gentiles—the ones who received this promise as outsiders. We can see ourselves as Peter. But we're also those who were on the outside looking in.

Our repentance, like Peter's, is a dramatic worldview shift, a vulnerable mindfulness that allows us to peer into God's eternal work through our lives. Our running to Jesus will ultimately have us running back to our neighbor.

In our roles as churches, then, we need to discern our own complicity in reinforcing the breakdowns in our world. In church specifically, we have deeply hurt others in the name of polity and policies and proof texted away God's image bearers—and this can be a way of avoiding the true tension required to love well. We are a part of the problem.

Healthy reflection will guide us in seeing how we collude in the world's divides and how we can hide behind our brand of ecclesiology. When we are confronted with our fear of others, a life of integrity would have us wrestle with our sacred texts— ever more vehemently—and not as an intellectual exercise. Our wrestling ought to be more like a joint enterprise with the Holy Spirit, in community, flowing through our hearts.

While this side of heaven we might see the limits of institutional inclusion on multiple levels, we can also be proximate to those left feeling rejected and hurting, and realize how the church institution reinforces it. Our rejection can be a form of violence, a story of trauma that people will carry in both body and soul for years to come. Are we doing our due diligence of discerning who might be included at that empty seat at the table?

More embrace is the ultimate goal, and more embrace can hopefully lead toward more mending. Yet meeting one another as God's beloved at the breaches of life requires daily submission and, as the apostle Paul would remind the church, even a daily crucifixion. Our fragmentation will continually bring us face to face with God, who will put us together again and send us back into the world. Never is the image of God clearer than when a disciple is vulnerable and repentant, and present to his or her own personal breakdowns and dis-integration.

God—the great inviter—then draws us, the church, into ever-deeper places of love. Places where heaven meets world, where God stands at the door knocking, calling, beckoning us to follow—promising to be with us through and through. This is not a deistic call, as with a nose pressed on the maternity ward glass, admiring children from afar.

Together we lean on an eschatological hope that God invites us forth like infants, and we will hearken, fresh out of the womb, to the familiar voice of a mothering God.

REFLECTION QUESTIONS

1. How has the calling of Christ led you to some aspect of learning disorientation?

2. What role has repentance played in your engaging others more lovingly?

3. What might Peter's continued disorientation in the Scriptures teach us about the nature of being a follower of Christ?

4. What will it take for our churches to live into a formation that "factors" disorientation as a natural part of growth?

5. How can developing the art of conversational skill be in-
   corporated into our process of discipleship? (For more resources, visit the Art of Hosting site: artofhosting.org.)

3

INCARNATIONAL
TRACING OUR EMBODIED FAITH THROUGH CHRIST'S BODY

Knowledge is only a rumor until it lives in the muscle.

SAYING OF THE ASARO TRIBE OF INDONESIA IN PAPUA NEW GUINEA

If we follow Jesus, we must follow him into the new patterns of embodied life that he enacted.

BRIAN BANTUM, *THE DEATH OF RACE*

OVER THE YEARS I've grown really fond of some good reality television. Especially those shows with amazing tattoo artists competing for cash prizes, with a magazine spread of the artist's works on display and a chance for a title that includes becoming the mother of all tattoo artists . . . if not in the whole world, at least in Brooklyn.

Through each round of competition the stakes are raised. Recipients of the tattoos are called human canvases. These brave volunteers will request a tattoo based on an image of their own liking. Each tattoo artist displays their best work, from tattooing portraits of deceased pets or family members to grayscale on a bald man's cranium to whole sleeves covering significant parts of a person's limb. In some instances, as if almost mystically, these tattoos meld with a person's body, displaying a fuller expression of a larger story to be told to the world.

Tattoo-ridden or not, our bodies will tell a story the moment we show up in this world. When we are first born, our bodies will be measured on a scale in pounds and ounces, perhaps telling the story of our health in utero. The color of our hair, its unfolding texture, our eyes, and our skin color will tell the story of our DNA, who our parents were, what parts of the globe our ancestors may have been from. As we grow, the variety of measures and scales will only expand. Our bodies will communicate all sorts of stories to the world. Our bodily stories will even be placed on the scales of judgment—on scales with unjustly determined value. Women will be judged according to their body types. Magazines will tout the perfect dimensions for the perfect facial structure. A person's skin color will lead to pre-told stories and scenarios before a person can even utter one word.

One question for the church today is, who gets to tell the stories of bodies in a world where the image of God in the human body is continually distorted?

Historically our lack of attention to a robust theology of the body has caused our faith to be out of harmony. Disembodied. Our theology has often been expressed through recited prayers, confessions, and doctrines with little emphasis on the incarnational aspects. Our ruminations about God and ministry can be disconnected from our actual lived experiences in our body and the bodily sufferings of a great many in our world.

A faith disconnected from the body is a faith out of balance. Today it's why many people find solace in Eastern traditions that bring the body into harmony. Here in the West, we've inherited a faith often maintained by confessional truths that can often remain in the realm of heady platitudes. Accordingly, embodying a faith that goes into the skin, tissue, bone, and marrow of human existence, based on the truth of the crucified and resurrected body of Christ, becomes the challenge of our day.

Our bodies are the fulcrum of our existence as human beings in the world. But we might find that we are largely unaware of the ways we experience the world through our bodies. For the sake of the world, churches need to redeem the practice of body awareness for a more integrated faith and a more robust discipleship. For the more aware we become of Christ's embodied actions, the more we can truthfully, discerningly, and effectively reimagine our own place in the world. We can exercise an honest, healing, and humble authority from this location.

We can begin to discern the path two ways: through (1) tracing our embodied faith through Christ's own body and (2) locating and discerning our embodied presence in the world.

ENCARNACIÓN: TRACING OUR EMBODIED
FAITH THROUGH CHRIST'S BODY

Speaking about Jesus as both God and human can ground a dis-embodied faith. God, in body, is written into the cosmic script, physically, in human flesh, dwelling at the intersection of heaven and earth. Jesus the begotten is the ultimate expression of seamless intersection: fully God, fully human, in a mystery we can't fathom.

It's known to us as the incarnation, and if read with Hispanic eyes, one can see the word *encarnación*, which carries better resonance for many of us, since *carne* is meat. This language forges images grounded in the body and keeps us from what Luis Pedraja calls "meatless" theologies.

Pedraja is quick to point out how much of our view of Christ has been left somewhere in the heavenly realms. He writes that "theologies without meat" (that don't take the human experience into consideration) are incomplete in light of Christ's life on earth. Pedraja writes, "It is still far easier to believe in a faraway spiritual reality than it is to face the realities of human life."

One of the exercises I've facilitated with groups to help integrate faith with the body is have them imagine Christ's presence through the image of silent black and white film reels, something reminiscent of the old Charlie Chaplin films. I guide people through a silent story focused on Christ's movements and messianic acts. In this exercise our focus isn't so much on the sayings of Christ in the red letters as much as his embodied movements in the Gospel stories.

I pick a story from the Gospels, or I invite them to pick a story, and ask, What might Christ's whereabouts communicate about his mission? Who is Christ in physical proximity to? What might it mean that he touched a leper or took the time to mix together spit and mud and physically touch a person's eyes? What does it mean that he allowed a woman to kneel as he reclined, to touch his feet and wash them with her tears? What did it mean for a woman with an issue of blood to touch Jesus? If we were to trace Christ's whereabouts, what would they say about his priorities? What do the places where Christ chooses to dine and recline say about his ministry? What does the permanent nature of Christ's scars communicate to us today? What about the actual geographical place of his crucifixion?

A faith disconnected from embodied ministry will shy away from these questions. On the other hand, for many who are exploring the faith, it can be an eye-opening venture—especially during a time when many of our churches are drawing skeptics or nominally religious people. Many are curious about the deeper questions of how the Christian faith connects to the concrete things of life.

Seeing the actions of Jesus emphasized as much as his sayings is potentially transformative. Christ's embodied acts allow for people to see him in daily mundane situations. We get to recover the most human elements of an incarnate Christ this way.

Many in my own church have asked how they can believe in a Christ resurrected in body. Or they might say, "I love your church, but I'm not sure about how Jesus can be God." Regardless of where a spiritual sojourner is regarding Christ's deity, the life of Christ remains compelling in the acts of his miraculous presence. Even many of the disciples doubted Christ's resurrection—until the work of the Holy Spirit began to make Jesus' reality more palpable after their bodies were baptized in the Spirit.

For seasoned Christians looking for a more tangible faith, talking robust, deep incarnation can become a second conversion experience. When people begin to see Jesus in more dimensional ways through his life in the world, they can also begin to see themselves in relationship to the world differently. They might even attempt to do some of the things Jesus did. They might find themselves located in space where they can interact with the world differently, under a different authority.

If we take the incarnation seriously, we will recognize that Jesus faced all of the realities of human life. It meant being tainted by the limits and lenses of people and their perceptions. Jesus inhabited all the social labels ascribed to him. In Christ's day, some would accept and some would reject him. Others would use his place of upbringing against him: "Is this not Jesus, the son of Joseph, whose father and mother we know? How can he now say, 'I came down from heaven'?" (John 6:42).

Jesus grew up a marginal first-century Jew from an obscure village in Galilee. As a baby, Jesus would be counted in the Bethlehem census. While in those days there was no ancestry software or mail order DNA vials to determine heritage, the book of Matthew (and thankfully, oral tradition) made it possible for us to trace Jesus' ancestry to human origins.

Under Rome, Jesus would be considered a noncitizen, out of the mainstream of Roman life. Jesus would walk. Weep. Jesus once sat thirstily at Jacob's well after his body grew tired. We can trace this same body to the Garden of Gethsemane, where he sweated heavily. His was a body with limits. Christ's body was scourged, nailed, and hung on a tree. And Christ's risen body was the same body that sat down with his disciples and ate a meal. The same body that bore the marks of existence here on earth— marks that will always, even in eternity, be traced back to a specific time, place, and memory in history.

The writer of Hebrews reminds us that when we attempt to locate this Christ, we physically move into places of disgrace and disinheritance: "So also Jesus suffered outside the city gate to make the people holy through his own blood. Let us, then, go to him outside the camp, bearing the disgrace he bore" (Hebrews 13:12-13). Orlando Costas says that we meet this Christ, crucified, outside the city gates, out in the places where we meet the poor and the marginalized, outside of the mainstream of Rome—in the underbelly of society.

Through Christ's bodily presence here on earth, we are compelled to see the image of God in both the marginalized and the ordinary. If Jesus' same narrative applied to life in America today, Jesus could've been mistaken for the guy preparing sandwiches in the back of the deli, doing bike deliveries for pizza places, or trimming someone's hedges. Andy Crouch writes that after the resurrection, the Bible points out how Mary Magdalene mistook Jesus for the gardener at his own gravesite: Jesus revealed within the image of human ordinariness.

In all the places that Christ would inhabit, he would honor the simplicity of humanity, participating in the ordinary, while performing signs and wonders pointing to a more transcendent reality than the one our world creates. In our formation as Christians it's important to know and trace the identity markers (e.g., ethnicity, race) of our own embodied lives in the world. Especially when identities are used to constrict us into being recognized as less than God's image bearers.

PRACTICE: TRACING OUR OWN EMBODIED PRESENCE IN THE WORLD

Incarnation is the lens through which we view our ministry intersection here in Harlem. For Mayra and me, this has been a key for being present in our neighborhood. In East Harlem we find ourselves in close proximity to two different subway lines. We're ten minutes from LaGuardia airport by car. And in a walking city, just five blocks north we can get some of the world's best and most famous soul food, at Sylvia's Famous, Amy Ruth's, or Spoon Bread. We can then walk a few blocks south and have some of the best and most inexpensive Puerto Rican and Dominican food.

Historically East Harlem has drawn immigrant populations. We love that there's an increasing Mexican presence in the barrio. Authentic Mexican food is probably the only kind of food my family can agree on. Meanwhile I try to convince my son that the franchise tacos he loves—the ones that double as cheeseburgers—have nothing on the authentic tacos next door or at the food cart. But alas, his discipleship has only begun.

We've become keenly aware of the history we inhabit here, rooted in struggle and renaissance. In the current so-called renaissance of gentrification we find that our multiple identities intersect with Harlem's history. Mayra and I are both from the "hood" historically. In many ways we represent the larger demographic of Latino/a and black here. We have also returned to the hood with education.

When we first showed up, our income was a few times the average, so we might have had a few more options than many. But this is all relative since the price of living in NYC in general causes money to evaporate like water on hot concrete.

We also wear labels in this world. These happen at the convergence of relative privilege and relative struggle in America. Our realities can wield both obstacles and opportunities for us to work toward flourishing, from the simplest everyday interactions to more significant ones.

For one, as a brown man, in the days before car services like Uber and Lyft, trying to hail a yellow cab in NYC was no small feat. I remember using Mayra's cache as a light-skinned woman. She would hail the cab, and I'd hop in out of nowhere and plop down in the back seat feeling like I'd won something.

At some tables, such as academic ones, Mayra carries some prestige as a tenured professor. In these same circles, she will also wrestle with numerous microaggressions from students or administration. She has often been mistaken for a student because some find it hard to believe she is faculty.

But I also see the Spirit's work through Mayra best displayed in the classroom, when she patiently walks with her students through unconscious bias. For fourteen years, over fifteen weeks each semester, she has made the invitation into racial awareness. She shows her students how our world will leverage their differences as a way of getting ahead or keeping others behind. She is exceptional at pointing out that differences do not need to divide us. Her indomitable awareness and resistance to bitterness in these places makes her a fierce peacemaker.

For peacemakers who stand at the breaches that divide people, becoming familiar with the language and the narratives assigned by our world is necessary for us to flip the script. We can't dismantle what we can't name. In doing this we become familiar with not only the scripts we're assigned, but also how we can stand at certain places of relative privilege in the world—the places where society attempts to locate us.

To the extent that a disciple is in tune with that reality, they can show up more conscious, wise, and present in the world. We can then enter any room and name or engage the potential pitfalls and politicizing of our presence, making ourselves more apt to "putting on Christ" and serving the world with distinction.

My own relative privilege showed up with me once at a community meeting in East Harlem. At the table were housing advocates working on informing a neighborhood rezoning process. Rezoning a neighborhood determines how communities are planned, where commercial space can be developed in relationship to residential space, how tall one can develop buildings, and how much affordable housing can be allotted, to name a few elements of a complex planning process. These advocates were people who lived in and represented the public housing developments. I was at this table realizing that I was one of them because I was Puerto Rican. Yet at the present moment my struggles were not the same struggles they had. I found myself very aware of my own educational and economic privilege. It wasn't until we connected around the collective struggle for affordable housing that fellowship began to take form. Only when I shared my own story, my own history and struggle, recounting my own experience with public housing, as well as my visceral knowing of the struggles of many within, did my presence become more influential.

This embodied narrative allowed me to sit more confidently and humbly before these powerful women. What's more, there was a glimmer in their eyes as if I were their own son, and hope for younger generations to continue to excel. A shift like this could not have occurred had I not been discerning my location in this forum.

Our embodied proximity to power, what we represent here on earth, is a political matter as well as a matter of being a follower of Christ. Our first citizenry and loyalty is to his kingdom, but the world will continue to have us jostle for position. Christ consistently will remind communities on "the underside" of how to be leaders in this world.

PEOPLE OF COLOR: THE POLITICS
OF EMBODIED PRESENCE

The embodied experience of many people of color in the world can be likened to the experience of the first-century exiles waiting on a conquering Messiah. Jesus knew this well, living as a Jew rooted in a history of exile, with a people time and again conquered by empires and kings. Each conquest brought new heralds with their own *euangelions*, gospels of "good news." Now, with the Messiah, the disciples could finally become a part of their own announcement and moment—the grand upheaval that would bring them out from under Roman domination. What would it feel like to no longer have the label of being the exiled, conquered, or colonized?

One day this led to an interesting conversation between James and John, the "Sons of Thunder," and their mother, who would make a particular request of Jesus, asking, "Grant that one of these two sons of mine may sit at your right and the other at your left in your kingdom" (Matthew 20:21).

Like any mother, she desired success and status for her children. She had a vested interest in their success and proximity to the power of King Jesus. Not only would it would distinguish them from among the Twelve but it would also set them apart. She knew that in their physical proximity to power, to be at his right hand and left meant to be given a special status and authority. After crushing Rome, they could receive the highest honor that came with conquest.

Jesus, who knew about the marginalized life outside of the mainstream, took these "I just can't wait to be king" moments as opportunities for conversation with his disciples about their own position in the world:

> You know that the rulers of the Gentiles lord it over them, and their high officials exercise authority over them. Not so with you. Instead, whoever wants to become great among you must be your servant, and whoever wants to be first must be your slave—just as the Son of Man did not come to be served, but to serve, and to give his life as a ransom for many. (Matthew 20:25–28)

Jesus showed that bodies—people's physical presence in the world—would be located and at times even dis-located by the powers of the world. But the priorities of God's kingdom would consistently challenge the social orders of our world. Christ the King, in holding space and physical proximity to those considered outcasts, touching those considered impure—the diseased, the lame, and the blind—and fellowshiping with foreign women, created a redemptive story for bodies, liberating them, breaking through the spiritual, social, and cultural categories that had served to imprison them.

Theologian Shawn Copeland describes further how this kingdom is embodied, writing,

> Jesus preached the *basileia tou theou*, the reign of God, as an alternative to the Pax [Peace] Romana; to put it sharply, he contrasted the future of bodies in God with the future bodies in empire. In every age the disciples must take up

his critique of empire and through *basileia* practice an incarnate alternative.

In a world where Caesar ruled with a "civilized," barbaric hand, Jesus encouraged his fellow Jews on the underside of conquest to show up differently. Disciples are an incarnate alternative when seated at the tables of power in the world.

"The last will be first."

"Do not take the place of honor."

"Whoever is least in the kingdom of heaven is greater."

Christ challenges the traditional seating charts at the tables and banquets of the world. The vision of Christ's banquet (on earth as it is in heaven) is one where people are serving one another, so much so that there's no room to focus on VIP and priority seating. There is no such category as first class or platinum or gold status to enter first. And even when a priority invitation is mentioned, Jesus says, "Bring in the poor, the crippled, the blind and the lame."

For people of color, whether we gain some form of economic advancement or a more central seat at the tables of our society, there comes a continual mandate for us to serve and uplift our communities, to show the world what a redeemed form of power looks like. Even when we find ourselves located in high positions and seats of prominence, we will constantly locate ourselves in lowliness in order to lift up others.

Christ's table in the social world will communicate ultimate reality. We live in this tension continually. And when we're able to contrast the tables of our culture with Christ's, we're able to embody the patterns of Christ at these intersections with power and grace, righteousness, and even resistance.

Aspects of this kind of table talk exist in our church life today, as we have Africans, black Latino/as, African Americans, and Afro Caribbeans worshiping together. I find it fascinating to see how Latino/as in particular see themselves, in their bodies, at the intersection of their presence and identity in the world. It has led to some provocative discussion on matters of how skin color creates its own hierarchy within my own ethnic group. This is referred to as *colorism*: the way people of color see themselves in light of blackness and whiteness and how they might benefit, or not.

In many cultures, the lighter one's skin, the more proximity to power one wields. The fairer the skin and the straighter the hair, and the more European characteristics worn on the body, the more one is seen positively in our world. Being a disciple of Christ in these contexts means becoming keenly aware of the enticements and entitlements that derive from a divisive color spectrum in our world.

In a conversation about this with one of our ministry coordinators, she inquired about why I had posted subject matter about Latino/as and blackness on social networking sites. This was a discipleship moment and an opportunity for her to share her personal experiences of colorism. Sabrina recounted growing up with her sister, who is darker skinned. Her sister was often told she was the ugly one of the two because her skin was a shade or two darker. As Sabrina recounted the story she became more aware of being treated with more attention and dignity simply because of her proximity to whiteness.

At one point Sabrina had tried to comfort her sister by saying that it doesn't really matter: "we are all black" anyway. I then mentioned to Sabrina that our sick society unfortunately deals on a racial spectrum (which is a sinful power). And countries in the Caribbean and Latin America have internalized this same cultural logic. I also pointed out how it's happening everywhere. Studies in our country have showed how girls with darker skin are suspended at three times the rate of other girls in high school, where "this uneven discipline is often the result of deeply ingrained racist and sexist stereotypes that push black girls out of school."

After our conversation I observed Sabrina feeling a renewed compassion for her sister. She could now, hopefully, become a more empathic ally. Moments like these will also raise consciousness for her as she works with children of color in a diverse setting, keeping her attuned to the narratives that work against them in our world. Embodied fellowship and solidarity will mean becoming a student of other people's struggles, so we can serve with nuance and distinction.

Just as the disciples had ambitions about their seat at the table, tensions remain between people of color in our society. Meanwhile a truism for personal identity runs parallel to one in real estate: it's all about location, location, location. Knowing where we are situated (and with whom we are situated) determines how we can more effectively engage the world.

Our identities as image bearers transcend the social labels we've been given. As the incarnation shows us, we live in a world where, though labeled, we can live through and even beyond our labels as light in the world.

When we've been toe tagged and are six feet under, people will not remember us simply for the markers that we were given by the world, but how we used our embodied selves to make an impact in the world. Whatever form of authority we've been given, wherever we find ourselves in society, we are always left with the question of how to wield this authority as the incarnate alternative of Christ located in a specific place in time.

Discerning our embodied location provides us a wisdom for engaging the world more effectively. We become one another's allies and advocates. We fellowship with one another at the intersection between shalom and the breaches of this world.

REFLECTION QUESTIONS

1. What do the embodied actions, miracles, conversations, and presence of Christ communicate to you about the gospels?

2. How is our view of power challenged when we read about Christ's view of leadership in Philippians 2:5-10?

3. Reflect on this quote by poet Rudy Francisco: "When you are the only black man in the whole neighborhood your skin is that one friend who meets everyone before you do." What story does this tell about skin and human bodies in many parts of the globe?

4. What do you discern your own embodied location (ethnicity, race, gender) to be in your context? At what "tables" do you hold some advantage? Disadvantage? How can you use these advantages to serve God's purposes?

5. What actions can you take to place yourself in proximity to, and arrange your life in such a way to learn more about, the struggles of other ethnic groups?

4

NAMING WHITENESS
DISCERNING SPACE AS DISCIPLE MAKING

Making room [for others] means knowing
how much room we take up.

DR. MAYRA LOPEZ-HUMPHREYS

Your attitude should be the same
as that of Christ Jesus.

THE APOSTLE PAUL

O N 135TH AND LENOX AVENUE in Central Harlem,
adjacent to Harlem Hospital, stands one of the city's
more unique public libraries: The Schomburg Center for Research in Black Culture. The Schomburg is named after an important yet little known figure of the Harlem Renaissance
named Arturo Schomburg.

Schomburg was born in the Virgin Islands to Maria Josefa, a free woman born in St. Croix, and Carlos Federico Schomburg, a merchant of German descent. In 1890 they would migrate to Puerto Rico and remain for a portion of Schomburg's life. While the details of his early life are limited, one narrative shaped his life's vocation.

One day in school his fifth-grade teacher said to him, "Los negros no tenían historia, ni héroes, ni logros" (Black people had no history, no heroes, no great moments). Her observation about having no great moments could be interpreted another way: having no record of being God's image bearers, leaving behind no contributions to culture and beauty in our world.

No doubt it was a jarring experience that would influence Schomburg's pursuits as a bibliophile and collector of artifacts across the world. He invested his life in proving to the world that African culture, black culture, had indeed contributed to beauty and history in the world, from the earliest days of civilization. While the collateral consequences of colonization meant the suppression of stories and contributions of other cultures, Schomburg's discoveries meant recovering a past long ago silenced.

Having lived in Harlem for over fifteen years now, I have developed an affinity for Arturo Schomburg. My research of Schomburg has led to some uncanny connections, many of which have helped me deepen and define my own identity as a black Puerto Rican in this world. For one, Schomburg embraced his own blackness as a Puerto Rican. He lived in a hybrid of cultures in ways that honored his mixed heritage.

Right around the time I was reading Schomburg's biography, Mayra gifted me with access to ancestry research online. In my search I discovered that my great-great grandparents on my father's side were from St. Croix. My great-great grandmother Carolyn was a free Cruxian (native to St. Croix) black woman. My great-great grandfather, George Humphreys, was born in St. Croix and was Irish, possibly descending from either Irish merchants or overseers (those who managed slave plantations).

According to immigration documents, George and Carolyn Johannes migrated from St. Croix in the 1870s to Puerto Rico. Their short journey, just less than fifty miles northwest, took them to the island of Vieques, where part of my Puerto Rican heritage begins.

Finding some commonality with a historical figure like Schomburg was a deep encouragement to me as I reflect the image of God in the world. Knowing there was a thinker out there who embraced his own interracial story normalized the angst I felt when not seeing enough of myself in the world. We descendants of the African and Afro Caribbean diaspora can go through life without seeing image bearers making significant contributions, without seeing others who bear our own physical likeness.

Many of these figures have been historically absent in our history books and museums. We see how only recently many here in the United States learned of three brilliant African

American NASA mathematicians named Katherine Johnson, Dorothy Vaughan, and Mary Jackson through a book-turned-movie, *Hidden Figures*. How many children have missed an opportunity to be inspired by the accomplishments of these three women?

This form of image bearing is so important. When people of color witness other people with beautiful dark skin making visible contributions—creating and contributing to culture and intelligentsia—it reminds us of our agency in the world. It can be a reminder of our creative capacity as children of God. We are here and no longer invisible.

Embracing my brown body and skin and recovering my own cultural heritage has made me a more whole and storied individual. My DNA holds the story of the struggle of conquered lands, peoples, and places, the mixing of races, histories, and cultures—even diaspora.

God continues to meet me at this intersection, forming the person who I am, doing work through me, helping others recover their own full identities in Christ. This is part of the reconciliation project, and by extension part of the ministry of our church. How can the histories of struggle and self-discovery be integrated into stories of our local church?

The church is entrusted with the ministry of being reconciled to God and one another. The way the church empowers people of color to exercise authority has been one of the greater contributions of some of the historical churches of color. This space must continually be claimed and reclaimed.

One of the challenges behind this endeavor is how church space is facilitated. How, if white people decide to join black and brown spaces, can they take on the posture of a learner? Discipleship in this endeavor becomes the practice of stewarding the spaces we occupy together across the cultural and racial spectrum.

How we include others, how different voices inform how we cultivate these spaces, matters. If church leaders of color faithfully and honestly name and challenge the white gaze in church spaces, while honoring our stories and our specific cultural contributions, it will be a gift to the world.

For our white brothers and sisters who are called to enter historically black and brown spaces, it will take deep interior work. It will take a revelation of how one's own embodied presence in the American experiment here and now is connected to America's history and story of racial power.

PRACTICE: DISCERNING THE WHITE
GAZE IN CHURCH SPACE

My discernment in naming the power of whiteness was often hampered by the start-up pressures related to church planting. We were operating at a frenetic pace. I was pursuing everything I could get my hands on toward a successful church start-up. If someone recommended a book, I read it. If there was a conference on starting churches, I attended it. If there was a learning cohort, I joined it.

One cohort in particular consisted of pastors and planters that would fly in from different parts of the country. At the time I was the only person of color in the group, as well as the only one local to New York City. Each meeting a consistent practice was to have us report our attendance numbers for the month with the question, "What are you running?"

Everyone around the table would report their attendance numbers. I remember always feeling some degree of shame that my church community had not broken some barrier of attendance. Part of this might have been rooted in my ego. But part of it was endorsed by a message that their way of defining and doing church was *the* way it ought to happen in the city. Somehow a small community was seen as a church that had hit a ceiling, or a church with some inherent deficit.

For years afterward I would often overlook the truth that we had a beautiful, diverse community actively engaged in loving God and the world. What we were doing and how it was happening by no means would produce explosive growth. Yet something dynamic was burgeoning while we were tilling the ground for a redemptive space.

Were people in this church plant cohort consciously trying to impose one way of thinking about church ministry in the city? I don't think so. Instead I surmise they really believed theirs was the default way, the normative way of doing church, because it produced the biggest and fastest results. In their unconscious assertions they leaned into market-driven ways of starting churches, without room or consideration for the perspectives of people of color. Meanwhile they had no idea how much space their white suburban perspectives were taking up.

I had internalized this story of church growth much earlier than this instance. Like many other pastors of color, I live within the tension of acknowledging the importance and value of my own perspective in the world of church health, while wrestling with certain fixations to feel validated within white circles. During certain times in my vocational journey, whiteness has played a disproportionate influence on how I've seen my contributions in the church world.

Just like a moviegoer who receives those oversized 3D glasses—mediating lenses through which we watch a film as the creators intended—only recently had I realized the deep influences whiteness has had on the world as I know it. Theologian Willie James Jennings describes this aptly when he calls whiteness "a facilitating reality" through which the world as we know it is viewed. Whiteness is a lens through which we learn to see and interpret the world around us.

In a world steeped in racial stories, we've inherited a mythology of whiteness—a story where whiteness has determined what is beautiful, what is valuable, what is sophisticated or excellent. To become aware of this lens is not to slight Western culture and all of its achievements. Instead it's the recognition of the deep limitations caused by humanity's misuse of certain gifts. It's also the acknowledgment that we need the resources of heaven and history to give us eyes to see and interrogate these stories and to ultimately dismantle single narratives from becoming dominant narratives that shape our realities as we know them.

The weapons of our warfare are recognition of the hidden, even unconscious stories we hold as graven images, influencing our behaviors, our actions, even our self-perception. This leads us to a vital question in our interrogation process: How might we discern the white gaze and its undue influence on our work in the world?

W. E. B. Du Bois describes the influence of this framing narrative, whiteness, as "this sense of always looking at one's self through the eyes of others." Church leaders need to take heed of how this gaze, this form of measure and judgment, has been internalized, and how it can become part of shaping our very identities as individuals. When the apostle Paul spoke to the church in Corinth he described the task of "demolish[ing] arguments and every pretension that sets itself up against the knowledge of God" (2 Corinthians 10:5). This form of spiritual warfare and story recognition takes prayerful discernment, reflection, and many, many conversations.

When I began to discern the white gaze and I realized how diversity itself had become my cool, sexy idol of affirmation, it led me to a place of disenchantment with the work of bridging racial divides. Somehow in this process I had been using the diversity of our church to falsely prop myself up. I was thinking, *If I can draw* [fill in the blank], *then I have become legitimate.*

The gaze of whiteness can pull at us, and if not confronted, it will make the voices "out there" have undue influence over us. In this respect, the need to prove, please, and pander runs deeper than a personality quirk. More, it reflects a deep insecurity that we are somehow less-than or unworthy. If unaware, we can hold deep-seated beliefs that our own Spirit-led inspiration, our creativity and vision, are to be doubted and even suppressed.

Discernment will allow us to see how the white gaze can shape our view of self as well as our contributions in the world. For people of color cultivating church spaces and cultures, this will mean recognizing how the white gaze influences the vocation of the body of Christ. In her book *The Elusive Dream: The Power of Race in Interracial Churches*, Korie Edwards describes how the diversity project in churches can fail if we remain unaware of how "hegemonic" practices play out in church cultures, and how in many ways churches will default to whiteness in the norms of how they operate. Edwards's research focuses on majority black and brown congregations with white people attending. Her research is sobering as well as an admonition for black and brown pastors who want to more effectively shepherd a multiracial and multicultural church movement.

Naming the white gaze will be part of many awakenings in our discipleship to dismantle white normativity and its influences on the church. The work of racial justice in church will partly be interrogating our unconscious biases, while acknowledging that racial dynamics exist and are deeply embedded into the fabric of reality as we know it. The white gaze can become less and less pronounced, less powerful, less influential, when our eyes become open to the truth that it exists.

The role of the pastor is to be discerning for the purposes of space making en route to the often-elusive vision of the beloved community. We can't internalize the mythologies that white people are the central cultural frame of reference. But to love is to participate in mutual embrace through honest conversation—the ultimate proximity that can lead to true, biblical repair of the breaches that divide.

FACILITATING CHURCH SPACE: CONVERSATION, EMPATHY, AND MUTUALITY

Mutuality and empathy are key fruit for the work of multiracial engagement. During my eleven-plus years as a pastor I have led many white brothers and sisters who are allowing the Spirit to work in their hearts as they show up in black and brown spaces. Leading in these formative spaces requires a vigilance to help people discern how to show up and participate in imagining a new form of belonging in the body of Christ. This form of belonging integrates mutuality and empathy to hold the stories that shape our struggle together while we rescript new counternarratives of church belonging.

The fruit of belonging and mutuality is how we all show up humbly in interracial spaces. For white brothers and sisters in black and brown contexts, it will mean taking on the posture of learners as well as divesting themselves of the power of white identity.

Philippians 2:1-8 provides us an anchor for our thinking about how we can strive to imitate Christ's "showing up" in the world. Paul writes,

> Therefore if you have any encouragement from being united with Christ, if any comfort from his love, if any common sharing in the Spirit, if any tenderness and

compassion, then make my joy complete by being like-minded, having the same love, being one in spirit and of one mind. Do nothing out of selfish ambition or vain conceit. Rather, in humility value others above yourselves, not looking to your own interests but each of you to the interests of the others.

In your relationships with one another, have the same mindset as Christ Jesus:

Who, being in very nature God,
  did not consider equality with God something to be
    used to his own advantage;
rather, he made himself nothing
  by taking the very nature of a servant,
  being made in human likeness.
And being found in appearance as a man,
  he humbled himself
  by becoming obedient to death—
    even death on a cross!

When Paul articulates the attitude of Christ through song, he is describing a disposition, Christ's posture for engagement with the world. Jesus, through the Spirit, enables humility, looking for ways to bridge breakdowns and fractures in creation. Ultimately it's this sacrifice that allows us, while attempting to sustain this servant nature posture and vantage point, even imperfectly, to remain in relationship together in more authentic ways.

In order to do this, pastors, leaders, and parishioners must become rooted in a Christ identity that honors culture and ethnicity, while exposing and subverting false narratives of power. Pastors are to pray, comfort, confront, and care for people beyond the color of their skin, but never remain unaware of the cultural maladies that dehumanize in a world that puts skin tone on an unholy spectrum.

Many people are craving a form of belonging beyond the narratives they've been given. In particular I have found that many of our white brothers and sisters are disillusioned by what they have witnessed (and continue to witness) in the white evangelical church. Many have yearned for a deeper vision of God's kingdom as represented imperfectly through the church. Over the years some have felt called to join our space, learning well these spaces can come with some cost.

Over time I have seen some disorientation as well as the fruit in journeying with white sisters and brothers. There were times I heard repeatedly, "I feel like the only white person in the church." Reflecting back, I don't believe it had to do with the number of white people present or not, or even the great amount of black and brown people in the room, but more how the culture of the community attempted to remain faithful to our black and brown context, honoring strong voices of color and the history of Harlem.

As we're in sincere fellowship together, many moments can be moments of awareness and empathy within the struggle to remain connected. Journeying together can shine forth moments of insight into our racialized world through deeper conversations, as they happen in real time. Our journey in this world is imbibed with many lessons for discipleship, through everyday conversations and incidental moments that can be converted to intentional spaces of healing.

One of these moments happened while I was traveling with my friend and leadership team member JJ in New England. We were returning from a meeting with some denominational leaders. On the way back to NYC we decided to stop at a diner in Connecticut. When we opened the door to the establishment, it was like something out of a movie.

At that moment it felt like the whole crowd of white diners just stopped their conversations, lifted forks from plates, refrained from eating, and gazed our way. JJ, feeling the awkwardness of the room, suggested we eat somewhere else. In many ways, he was being protective as well. I refused and said, "I want to stay because I believe in the ministry of exposure," emphasizing how important it is to challenge spaces, bringing moments of disruption to white gazes, even by simply deciding to eat in a place where the hospitality is lacking.

Merely by our presence, JJ and I created a table of communion at this diner—because of our agreement to do faith together. This is a snapshot of what the larger table of heaven will look like, and it is a form of resistance to homogenous places. JJ and I were able to process this moment on the way home. He asked, "Don't you know what some of these folks might've thought of you?" In other words, "Were you not aware of what the gaze communicated?"

For JJ, the formative moment consisted of cultivating an empathic imagination—empathy for people of color who daily occupy inhospitable spaces in the world. It is in this identification with disinheritance (be it momentary disinheritance or perpetual) that the church can become the church.

In *Bonhoeffer's Black Jesus*, Reggie Williams describes this empathic moment: "Christ is present in the world as the church, in the communion of saints, in the community of believers. Christ existing as the church is empathic, vicarious, representative action." Empathic action can bring us toward deeper imagination for our fellowship together—celebrating with one another, developing a capacity for intimacy with others that we otherwise would not think possible. Together we experience a reconstitution of identity that is both actual in Christ yet also progressively forming.

An empathic imagination, an imagination cultivated through walking with others in their stories of hurt and rejection, cultivates a posture for friendship. For a pastor of color though, the empathic imagination can be cultivated toward white people who are de-centering whiteness in search of living a new identity in Christ.

What is the consequence of living a narrative that places a person and their white skin color at the center, as *the* frame of reference for the world? What kind of dehumanization does this enable? Imagining this became a little less of a challenge when I revisited my own cultural heritage story. A story that has taught me, erroneously, how men are at the center, more valued than and superior to women.

In my own marriage I held unconscious beliefs about women rooted in machismo. If it were not for numerous conversations—and my fits of anger and annoyance at feeling my maleness displaced from the center—I wouldn't have realized the extent of how hostile this world could be to women. Through her life, my partner, along with many other sisters in Christ, has shown me how men can exercise a dampening, diminishing form of authority. I've witnessed how this has affected my wife and countless women who are equally image bearers in the eyes of God.

Developing empathic imagination will mean arriving at a different vantage point, away from false identities based on this world's hierarchies. This imagination will be shaped by the cross of Christ—Christ's presence extended in love in vulnerable and open presence. When we follow Christ on this trajectory we are compelled to show up differently, making room for others to do the same.

At times pastors will have moments or forums where these dynamics can be discussed openly. Moments such as these won't happen every day, but they may also simply be a cup of coffee away from happening if we're open. Seeking and receiving these space-making moments will continually challenge everyone involved in a church community. Especially when white sisters and brothers have a sincere call to serve in black and brown spaces. I count conversations like these with non-black/brown parishioners as redemptive moments.

One of the more formative conversations happened with my brother David at a local cafe. David works in commercial real estate and had been visiting our church for about one year. He had come from a larger church on the Upper East Side of Manhattan. But his life had been more immersed in communities of color, and he was experiencing a change in his heart and perspective, drawing him to join a different space for worship and fellowship.

He asked, "Is there room for me as a white male from the business world in this church community? Is there room for me at Metro?"

David's question was a challenge to my imagination about our church. My preaching had been geared toward affirming people of color in the image and likeness of God, or encouraging justice-minded white people to exercise a prophetic voice to dismantle the stronghold of racism in the world. But I had been missing elements of hospitality, challenge, and integration beyond those realities. Was I truly committed to pastoring and discipling people from different experiences? The pastoral call to show up in the gaps this way is a particular call to journey with others. But if we allow Christ to do his work in tandem with sisters and brothers like David, it will begin to heal pastors of color as well, enlarging their souls as they continue to make room at the table.

From that moment a challenge was birthed for David in naming how his showing up and staying could influence a small church. How he chose to stay would be an exercise in disorientation and discomfort at times. It would require holding back certain opinions and realizing how the weight of his words in *our context* could carry a different impact because of how social status plays out in the world. But David was not just committed to doing the internal contemplative work; he was committed to learning and doing life together with our community.

Our commitment together was to remain open to God's work so we could grow in fellowship together. Our common tract was the grace and humility of Christ's Spirit within us. David has also performed a very countercultural work not found enough in many white evangelical circles. He has allowed himself to remain under the leadership of a person of color.

Over the years, David has served as our church's board chair and is one of our most trusted leaders. I officiated his wedding and have dedicated his children. We've truly become brothers in every biblical sense of the word. Yet in truth, the journey for me, for our church, has been challenged with more losses than gains in the area of reconciliation. Sustaining great momentum when it comes to growing and integrating more of our white sisters and brothers has not come without some exits, for a range of reasons, for sure.

What I do hold in my memory are snapshots, which to me are signs of light and the gaze of heaven's hope. Signs are impermanent moments where I've seen glimpses of the kingdom of God repairing the breaches through the church. These are not monuments to multiethnic ministry that celebrate the aesthetics—or as I heard someone once say, "The multiple colored jelly beans in the jelly bean jar." I don't believe God is satisfied with that reality; God desires more from the church even when it costs her.

While racism and white supremacy continue to be a footnote in each chapter of the American church, affecting and shaping the American consciousness, the church has been called to a counternarrative. To become aware of the places of privilege that come from racism and the impact of the white gaze is to become aware of the form of warfare the church is waging. To name the idols, the framing metaphors, the stories that constitute our understanding of how whiteness has become the normative story, is to begin the process of tearing down imaginations and anything that sets itself against the knowledge of God.

Being the church together will never be a one-sided work. But as Jew and Gentile have come together to form a new humanity, we, as children of God, separated by the strongholds of race in our world, must once against foster an empathic imagination, together realizing how we have all been dehumanized by this story of racism. In our day the image of Christ will never be more apparent than in a diverse community, and never more deeply demonstrated than when we can name and dismantle the walls of hostility that divide us, naming the gazes that loom over our Christianity in North America.

In diverse church spaces, then, this must be a consistent intention in claiming the spaces we're cultivating together, where voices are honored and heard as integral to the mission itself. One question that can prove to be a guiding light is, How are we willing to come together around this compelling gospel vision with a big table for all of God's children? The measure of the signs and wonders of such a heavenly vision is not so much how long we stay together, but how moments together provide snapshots of God's kingdom, moments where our collective realities together become God's.

It will require an attitude like that of Christ—that is, self-emptying, projecting the image of Christ in humility, whether it means increasing one's presence or decreasing as it is discerned.

Crosscultural engagement will require that we love ourselves fully in our God-given humanity. When I'm in community with my white brothers and sisters it is imperative that I come fully engaged with the dignity of an image bearer. Anything less would dishonor the image of God in me, and them as well. We ultimately dishonor one another when we exclusively place one another on a racialized foundation, which translates into sinking sand.

REFLECTION QUESTIONS

1. How might our church reflect the racial dynamics and divisions of the world we live in?

2. What gospel-based conversations are in place to discuss the dynamics of privilege as tethered to whiteness in our church today?

3. For persons of color, how might our work be influenced by the gaze of whiteness?

4. How can our church space better represent a range of aesthetics, gifts, creativity, and insights of different cultures?

5. What does our preaching and teaching say (if anything) to the larger community about the insights and opinions of authors, theologians, and writers of color?

6. How might sincere compliments and feedback from a white person carry more weight than those of persons of color in our church context?

7. For further consideration: How are we discerning the complexities of intersectionality? (That is, the interconnected complexities of overlapping identities: disability, race, class, gender, etc.) Multiple identities can overlap, and people can be overlooked as a result (e.g., a white woman bypassed for promotion because of gender considerations).

PART 2

STAYING PUT

5

STAYING PUBLIC
WELCOMING HOME
THE PROPHETS

You are a story. Do not become a word.

NAYYIRAH WAHEED

ONE OF THE BEST EULOGIES I've ever heard was not at a funeral, ironically, but in a Netflix show about Hell's Kitchen's hero, *Daredevil*. A Roman Catholic priest named Father Lantom eulogized a violent neighborhood gangster named Elliot Grote after a street vigilante named Frank Castle killed him.

When it came time to memorialize Grote, no one attended his funeral except three people who had barely known him. Not one family member, not a coworker. No one.

All of the different parts of his relational ecosystem were conspicuously absent. Father Lantom moved forward with his eulogy, saying, "Elliot Grote was no saint. He was human. Deeply flawed." He then recalled how Grote attended church every

Sunday, "friendless and alone. Right there in that pew." Grote was described as a gangster by day who would sit in the pews seeking a redemption that somehow never came.

According to Father Lantom, "He died alone with no one to mourn." Even without much good to find in Grote because of the path he had chosen, Father Lantom reaffirmed something that is true of all image bearers connected to the larger creation: "One person is not just one person. In each of us there is a world webbing out, reaching others. Creating reactions—sometimes equal, sometimes opposite. We rush to say one life is gone, but each of us is a world. And today a world has been lost."

Father Lantom described Elliot Grote as a world reaching out, placing him and his humanity in a web of relationships. And because of Grote's untimely exit from earth, perhaps he and others now missed out on the redemptive possibilities of his world.

As image bearers of God our Creator, every human being is a world unto himself or herself, and every image bearer is wired for the possibility of mending tattered relationships and bringing beauty and flourishing into their personal and public life, creating actions and reactions in the world around us. We were created to take up space in the universe! And our taking up space comes with specific purpose, as redemptive possibilities are all around us in both the personal and public sphere, making our gospel more generous than we perhaps have ever known it to be.

A single-dimension gospel that focuses mainly on our personal life will otherwise be a stingy, narrow gospel that doesn't take into consideration that people are worlds unto themselves.

It will be a gospel lacking language or imagination for God's healing hand within a divided world.

Christians have all been taught a language for this gospel, whether it was caught by default or intentional by discipleship. Therefore one key question is, how does the language of the good news we profess shape our understanding of the church's place in the world?

What if we taught people a language of a gospel of shalom large enough to weave together the breakdowns between the personal dimensions of faith and the more interpersonal? What if we began to revisit the dimensions of the Christian story in such a way that it comes alive to others in every dimension in life: social, emotional, bodily, and cognitive? A whole gospel can sound heretical to its own hearers and adherents because it will challenge the traditional ways we tell the story. These conversations can even push people to the cliff-side edges.

We all long for a gospel story grand enough to deal with the complexities of a world looking to integrate faith more fully. If not, the church will continue to turn in on itself. Without spaces for dialogue we can lose our discipling rigor. The church will not become a sacred place for the practice of Christian conversation without a more expansive biblical language to engage the world across the spectrum of "personal salvation," cultural engagement, and public witness.

This task is partially theological. When Christians begin incorporating the language of shalom it can make for a more holistic approach to the gospel. Our minds will need to be trained into a new language, grounded in the concrete realities of our day.

Revisiting our theology within our gospel is a worldly risk, but as a church, it can help us stay together and stay public in two ways: (1) by expanding the language of our gospel through a deeper understanding of shalom and (2) by naming concrete practices and opportunities to make the connections between shalom and action in real time.

THE STORY OF SHALOM: HARMONIZING PERSONAL AND PUBLIC FAITH

In my years of church ministry in a diverse setting, the best metaphors to communicate the integration of personal and public faith have come through a jazz infused, shalom gospel theology. Metro Hope has always been a movement inspired by jazz. Yes, it is true that churches absorb some of the quirks of their founders—but we have often found jazz to be an appropriate metaphor, honoring how the church community can resemble the best parts of it.

With pastors as facilitators of the church as an ensemble community in creative tension, encouraging people to find their voices in an ever-expanding reality, we can learn how our simple gospel "standard" can engage the complexities of the world that we live in, in both personal and public life. In his book *Resurrection City: A Theology of Improvisation*, Dr. Peter Heltzel writes about the church in jazz terms:

> I believe Christian thinking and *social witness* can be understood analogously with jazz music. Like jazz, Christianity is a dramatic and musical performance. Like jazz,

Christian thinking and acting are improvisational, creative
and hopefully forward-looking. Like jazz, they exemplify a
dynamic of constraint and possibility. Constrained by the
norm of God's word, Christians seek to creatively engage
their world in light of the Word. In their work and witness,
Christians use the material at hand—principally the language and example of the prophets and Jesus in the context
of their life—to creatively riff for justice, love, and shalom
in the present and thereby open up a new future.

Heltzel presents the beautiful image of shalom as seamlessly
weaving together a robust vision of personal faith with heavenly
glimpses of what could happen when this faith goes public in
its witness.

Reminiscing over my own Latino/a Pentecostal church experience, I remember witnessing signs and glimpses of this form of
shalom. I have never experienced the beauty of intergenerational worship, a mutuality found in honoring our elders, a passionate love for Christ, and a desire to witness to others about
God's transforming love more than I did in this space.

In the Latino/a church, personal passion for Christ was paramount, as well as the unity of the Spirit. Our harmony was expressed in deep community and togetherness, which was our own
personal snapshot of what heaven felt like. I remember the night
before our epic church picnics our little kitchen full of sounds of
clanking pots and canola oil crackling on the stovetop. Mami
would be seasoning chicken with the Goya seasoning Adobo, our

universal condiment. The next morning, wood-paneled Chevy wagons double parked at the rendezvous point at church. Groups of children would crowd in the back of hatchbacks with open windows and optional seatbelts. Minor details would never get in the way of a good church picnic.

We rolled out together and that's what mattered. I recall a feeling of deep belonging. Somehow deep within my eight-year-old self, things were pleasant and wonderful. Unity seemed easier in this first-generation Latino/a church. It only grew complicated when younger generations began to question the personal expression of their faith in public settings. These folks couldn't understand why there were such dividing walls between them and the culture of the world.

Like dated milk, the language of faith began to expire, with younger generations interrogating the language and metaphors of holiness. The language of "in the world, but not of the world" became isolationist and elitist. In the midst of this language deficit, community became unraveled. When our church community was faced with these threats it began to batten down on its beliefs. With no spaces (or know-how) for healthy conversation, we found that our road trips together happened less and less. A good group of us stood at the edge. Some of us were pushed out, and others left on their own, with others jettisoning church altogether.

Many of our pastors were brilliant, even with limits in formal education in this country. They were facing first-generation complexities—doing the best they could. We must realize how the cultural questions a first-generation church is responding to will often be in contrast to those of subsequent generations. With generational complexities it is indeed difficult for churches to avoid "holes" in their gospel when attempting to engage faithfully. But the disorientation of reclaiming, refreshing, and recapturing language is real and vital.

The church will turn in on itself without space for finding fresh biblical ways of imagining and communicating our precious story. And many will continue to view the church as having lost its prophetic edge (hence its social impact). The church will be known as a chorus of echoes with no room for harmony—which is defined by the Oxford Dictionary as "the combination of simultaneously sounded musical notes to produce chords and chord progressions having a pleasing effect."

What happens when the church goes beyond echoing a biblical message diluted by American individualism or denominational tribalism? While lifting up the voices of the prophets, the voice of Christ calls the church back to loving God *while* also loving people in faithful public witness. Shalom-makers who attempt to practice and harmonize the message will find themselves following an improvisational Messiah who could be interpreted as offensive—even to many of his followers. This Christ would carry, embody, even fulfill the same tradition as the Old Testament prophets, individuals who would publicly engage people and systems that had fallen short by neglecting the disinherited, neglecting God's law of love.

Prophets as God's spokespersons could be real irritants this way, which can be a challenge to the church as well. Church is often a space where the majority of people want their sermons neatly packaged, with the service ending on a glorious high note.

But Jesus didn't seem to be into neatly packaged teachings. Many people today should wrestle with texts like Luke 4, where Jesus opens the scroll in Isaiah and reads,

> The Spirit of the Lord is on me,
>> because he has anointed me
>> to proclaim good news to the poor.
> He has sent me to proclaim freedom for the prisoners
>> and recovery of sight for the blind,
> to set the oppressed free,
>> to proclaim the year of the Lord's favor. (Luke 4:18-19)

The gospel of Luke relates how Jesus' hearers were amazed and impressed at his words, though it was probably a text familiar to many. And when I read this story I almost hear myself saying, "Jesus, stop right here. Just leave the people encouraged and inspired—now's the perfect time for a mic drop. Just do the altar call!" But instead Jesus would go into other business:

> "Truly I tell you," he continued, "no prophet is accepted in
> his hometown. I assure you that there were many widows
> in Israel in Elijah's time, when the sky was shut for three
> and a half years and there was a severe famine throughout
> the land. Yet Elijah was not sent to any of them, but to a
> widow in Zarephath in the region of Sidon. And there were
> many in Israel with leprosy in the time of Elisha the

prophet, yet not one of them was cleansed—only Naaman the Syrian." (Luke 4:24-27)

What was Jesus doing? Jesus was fulfilling Scripture. The gospel of jubilee would now be a public venture reaching out to the world of the Gentiles. This is also where Luke records a mob from Jesus' hometown bringing Jesus to the brow of a cliff to be pushed over, with Jesus somehow becoming elusive.

Even the Son of Man knew the challenge of starting with a community he would no longer be welcome in. People, after all, don't take kindly to others shifting the safety of their worldviews, nor will they welcome the accompanying disorientation. Truthfully, this is the type of irritation that can lead anyone to want to push out a prophet. Our hearts are not nimble, or perhaps our imaginations are too narrow to receive such a scandalous gospel that reaches and pushes out so far. The gospel is for everyone personally, yet is also beyond just us. The gospel will always be working through our personal worlds and reaching out to other people in their worlds, seeking redemptive possibilities.

This is why prophetic imagery like that of shalom is important, because it encompasses what happens when Christ's kingdom is at work in the world and moving forward in its fulfillment. Shalom provides a word picture that jars our theological imaginations. Perhaps we have thought of shalom as peace and have associated it with serenity or the absence of conflict. But shalom is active. It embraces a complex world where we witness ruptures and traumas in both the personal and public spheres of life. The seekers of shalom, the children of God, will continually strive toward God's alternative vision of a world turned whole and upside down.

Author and activist Lisa Sharon Harper captures this sense of shalom where heaven's intent converges with the world's people and systems:

> Shalom is what God declared. Shalom is what the Kingdom of God looks like. Shalom is when all people have enough. It's when families are healed. It's when churches, schools, and public policies protect human dignity. Shalom is when the image of God is recognized in every single human. Shalom is our calling as followers of Jesus's gospel. It is the vision God set forth in the Garden and the restoration God desires for every relationship.

Shalom can ignite people's imagination to envision what life looks like when it's very good, which was God's declaration on the sixth day of creation. Good in every sense though—not just for our own tribes, but an all-encompassing flourishing for the good of the entire world. Shalom can also steer us out of the realm of theological and ecclesial divisions. With Christianity historically plagued by liberal/conservative debates, with the language of a social gospel off-putting to conservatives, and with liberals weary of evangelicals often focusing too narrowly on public engagement, the song of shalom can locate the church as reclaiming a more expansive role as peacemaker. Shalom is a harmonious voice consistently attuned to justice, creating space in the church for the prickly prophets in our midst.

PRACTICE: NIMBLE JUSTICE AND
HONORING THE PROPHETS AT HOME

The apostle Paul reminds us that the influences and the gifts of the apostles, prophets, pastors, teachers, and evangelists work together in harmony for the building up of the church in the world. The church's holy quintet seamlessly prepares its people for God's work in the world, building the church from the inside, preparing it for public ministry in the Spirit of our Messiah.

The work of the church is to cultivate prophetic voices as one vital expression of the church's public face in the world today. Pastors will find only a small portion of these voices inside the church, because they're out there. We might find some people who don't connect to church in traditional forms, such as Sunday service hospitality, greeting, and worship. But burning within them is a heart for God's people to return to see God's mending justice in the world.

My friend Stephen Tickner fit this profile early in the life of our church. Stephen once mentioned how he couldn't connect to Christ through music and songs of the church. Instead, he felt closest to God when serving the interests of the poor. He felt more connected to God when pondering God's presence at the breakdowns of our society. There he clearly saw Jesus as the companion of the poor, with Stephen's involvement expressed as a most holy act of worship.

As a new pastor at the time I had to discern how to best support Stephen's journey. Far be it from me to quench the soul of Stephen's own quest. So together we discerned Stephen heading our justice-shalom ministry. In that capacity Stephen was able to recruit a team and over one year facilitate more than twenty-five new connections and collaborations between our church and other churches, faith-based organizations, intentional communities, and seminaries, getting our people involved in the formative work of justice in our community.

Stephen would also join an organization called NYFJ, which worked to mobilize clergy and laity around unjust policies contributing to poverty and food insecurity in NYC. Stephen's search for a more whole faith would eventually lead him to seminary, where many of us witnessed his transformation—his faith didn't just remain public, but he also became a person with a renewed passion for the biblical text.

I have found time and time again that when we become open to a renewed and expanded understanding of the gospel it becomes a second conversion. When people move with Christ into more places in the world the good news becomes amplified. Meanwhile the generous boundaries of God's graces are infinitely wider than many could ever hope for. Every dimension of life hence becomes a mission, where God's shalom is extended toward repairing the breaches.

Preparing our parishioners to exercise public faith doesn't necessarily require the development of new church programs. Our churches can instead be vicariously represented throughout various justice intersections. Our church and our faith in the world can be nimble and responsive this way.

A gospel of shalom will be foundational for a personal and public movement where leadership consistently teaches the seamless connections between each ministry opportunity as a formative practice of faithful discipleship. Formative public ministry is teaching people to be prayerfully responsive to the world around them, in real time.

I recall when our church encouraged our people to forgo attending Sunday service in favor of being in solidarity at a rally in DC on behalf of Dreamers and the undocumented. From the pulpit we framed it around Rabbi Abraham Joshua Heschel's moment with Dr. King in Selma in 1965. Rabbi Heschel famously integrated contemplative conviction and public and prophetic witness when he said, "I felt like I was praying with my feet." We also made connections to the Old Testament Scripture that reads, "The foreigner residing among you must be treated as your native-born. Love them as yourself, for you were foreigners in Egypt. I am the LORD your God" (Leviticus 19:34).

A similar moment of nimble justice came after the earthquake in Haiti in 2010. I found there was no greater moment to connect artistic and intellectual energies and other gifts from within the church. Our Hope for Haiti event had us integrate the talents of artists, vocalists, poets, musicians, and academics. At the time we had one of CNN's correspondents become a part of a panel on the state of Haiti. Being part Haitian himself, he participated in a forum that was both personal and informative to raise awareness about the situation on the ground as it developed.

Responses to disaster can often feel like drops in the ocean, but this is what makes our collective responses acts of faith. Our faith journey continually reminds us of how our minute efforts are merely drops of water in the ocean. Yet our goal is not to be messiahs in the world, but to perform acts that can bear witness to God's presence in the world through God's church.

An African proverb wisely reminds us, "If you think you're too small to make a difference, try spending a night with a mosquito." Light shines through when we remember how small contributions are part of a collective cultivation in the rooting of God's commonwealth. Our collective scratches on the heavenly chalkboard screech for justice loudly together.

I've witnessed some growth moments as well. One of our worship leaders, Eurice, had mentioned how she felt her singing voice that day was more than just personal worship. Hope for Haiti connected her powerful voice in worship to a public matter in Haiti. It became more than disaster relief. For Eurice, this was a discipleship *touch point*: her spiritual growth came in weaving together the personal and public dimension of faith, connecting her voice on 125th Street to the many voices unheard in Haiti.

If public faith is about partnering with God and others, joyfully inviting beauty, flourishing, harmony, and redemption into our world, then there is purpose to be found. If all activity—art, writing, parenting, gardening, marriage, and so on—is about contributing to flourishing, then there is purpose to be found. A single protest, speech, policy analysis, or haiku about God's work in the world can be a medley of shalom-filled efforts pointing in the same direction. Engagement of this form can never be reduced to being mere charity, but is rather incarnational expression.

Our people can integrate personal and public faith when they recognize that worship is also connected to God's concern for the world, with every person a world reaching out as part of God's ecology of grace. Teaching a gospel of shalom gives us a bigger story from which to draw, with language and imagery that allow us to cross boundaries where perhaps gospel language has fallen short.

Shalom will continuously be outward facing, beginning in the family of faith and trickling out into the world. Being known as shalom-makers is a collective formation and a form of discipleship requiring personal devotion and public witness, elements that are crucial for people staying together. Heralding and embodying this good news will be the church's performance. The church will then need to practice as it finds its voice in the world.

With this improvisational and adventurous message the church might find itself at the intersection that Dr. Gabriel Salguero calls "between Hope and Hades," at the edge with the prophets with the threat of being pushed out of a limited evangelicalism as it adopts Jesus' Jubilee platform. We can indeed reclaim a space where the priesthood of believers, with their distinct gifts and voices, join together in witnessing to the nations.

REFLECTION QUESTIONS

1. Considering how "everyone is a world" connected to a larger ecology, how do you attempt to harmonize personal and public witness in your Sunday messages?

2. What about your gospel language needs to be revisited? How might its focus be too internal (for example, limited to the soul)? How might it be overly externalized (for example, with a focus on evil systems or demons and angels)?

3. How has your church established a public presence in its neighborhood beyond the church building?

4. How might we be ignoring the prophetic voices in our church?

5. What opportunities might be available to connect the gospel message in the church with specific actions outside the church as a public witness?

6. How have you or your church been pushed to the margins (with the prophets) lately because of your heart for God's shalom in the world?

6

REMAINING AT WORK
BECOMING GOD'S CROWDSOURCE IN THE BARRIO

We're known as a small church that
leaves a big footprint in the city.

**RUTH EVON IDAHOSA,
EXECUTIVE DIRECTOR OF PATHFINDERS**

METRO HOPE CHURCH rents space from Harlem's historic National Black Theater. We're located just off 125th Street, Harlem's main corridor. On Sundays, this little corner of Harlem can feel like a religious food court experience. We share space with other churches and even cults—the church of Scientology meets adjacent to us. We "fight" for signage space while churches display their wares for tourists seeking a true Harlem experience. We're like information booths for purveyors of gospel choirs and smothered chicken.

On any given Sunday you might hear me say, "Welcome to Metro. We're grateful you made us your stop today. If you feel your experience is lacking here, you can head on over to Mount Moriah Church—they have a gospel choir just across the hall— but just remember, they won't serve you glazed donuts with fair trade coffee . . ."

Well, if I don't say it, I'm thinking it.

But despite my occasional cynicism, I'm convinced Metro's presence and staying power is vital to our community. What was once a great adventure in "What's the point of another church in Harlem?" has rooted and defined our distinctive reach into the very arteries of our community. It has been a slow, long journey in a city where only the most resourced survive. Yet in working in a rapidly changing context like East Harlem, we position ourselves in a posture of prayer and discernment, seeking clues about the gifts others bring. We are open to God working through others to shape our collective vision and vocation, acknowledging how every person brings gifts that can further God's enterprise in the world.

DISCERNING GOD'S AGENDA FOR OUR WORK

The people that have come to and through Metro are mainly human service professionals, artists, and small business entrepreneurs. "Selling" our folks on the notion of compassion and justice work has never been the great challenge. The greater endeavor is showing through the Scriptures how our work is tethered to God's concern for people and places in the world.

In the Holy Scriptures, Jesus, in some sense, invents the role of workplace chaplain. "Come, and I will you make fishers of men," is a sacred invitation wrapped in vocational metaphor. In his work as a rabbi, Jesus encountered tanners, Pharisees, tax collectors, and centurions. In the beginning of his ministry his base of operation was the little town of Capernaum, where James, John, Andrew, and Peter had homes and small fishing businesses.

Jesus' enigmatic stories would draw from images of agrarian labor, giving kingdom lessons that even included questionable businesses practices (see Luke 16:1-13). Those enigmatic stories were loaded with deep contrasts between the work of the children of light and those who were known to extort the poor.

Luke's gospel recounts a time when Jesus walked through Jericho. On the path he sees a tax collector named Zacchaeus propped on a Sycamore tree, attempting to get a view of a popular rabbi named Jesus. To Zacchaeus's surprise, Jesus approaches and calls him down. And even more astonishing, Jesus invites himself over for dinner. As if this audacious rabbi's gesture wasn't enough, it couldn't overshadow the fact Jesus would be dining with a tax collector, a profession mired in deep controversy in first-century Israel.

Jesus' encounter with a tax collector was a connection to the Roman Empire's system of taxation. A friendly encounter with Zacchaeus would understandably leave any Jew embittered. According to Talmudic Law, tax collectors were thieves who extracted wealth from local communities as stewards of the Roman

Empire. People serving in this role were also known to be pred-
atory lenders, giving money to those unable to pay, creating a
system of private debt with interest. It's no wonder Jesus' association with Zacchaeus could be considered scandalous.

Knowing full well what sharing a table with Zacchaeus meant,
Jesus engaged the controversy nonetheless. And what happened
next would tell the story of true redemption. Zacchaeus responded
to Jesus' hospitality in a transformative way. His allegiance to
Rome, and his own pockets, would be supplanted by a new allegiance to Christ's kingdom. And Zacchaeus's deep repentance led
to a deep shift in how he would steward his work in the world.

Instead of extracting and exploiting wealth from his community, he proposed to seek economic *flourishing* and restorative action, saying, "Look, Lord! Here and now I give half of my
possessions to the poor, and if I have cheated anybody out of
anything, I will pay back four times the amount" (Luke 19:8).

Salvation led to a redefining of his stewardship and his work
in Jericho. For Zacchaeus, it wasn't necessary to join rabbi Jesus
on the itinerant path. Instead he would remain a disciple in a
despised profession, reflecting the image of a just Creator. Zacchaeus would locate God's activity through his work in the world.
There was no question here that Zacchaeus's salvation would
lead to a concrete impact on the local economy in his neighborhood. One can only imagine Jericho would not be the same.

Looking at the Zacchaeus story in this way provides deeper
questions about how our work can reflect the image of God. For
one, how is our salvation through Jesus the animating force for

our work in the "here and now"? What happens when the image of God reflected in our good work puts us in tension with larger systems of darkness in our world?

One of our parishioners named Evon was confronted with this decision in her own vocational journey. She came to Metro as a defense attorney and was at the cusp of making partner at her firm. Yet Evon was wrestling at a crossroads of discerning her vocation in a new season.

"Pastor, the messages at Metro have me considering leaving my law practice to start a nonprofit."

I thought to myself, *That's crazy talk. What is it with people at Metro and their vows of poverty?* Sigh. "Evon, that sounds great. How can we get on God's agenda for your work?"

Evon would eventually leave her law practice to start Pathfinders, a NYC-based nonprofit that works internationally as an advocate for women who are victims of human rights violations. She was instrumental in putting together the Bring Back Our Girls campaign after an extremist faction called Boko Haram kidnapped 276 girls in Nigeria in 2014. Her work in Nigeria can place her in precarious situations, even to the point of personal safety concerns.

Not one year into her work, Evon was selected from a list of distinguished honorees as one of New York's New Abolitionists. No doubt this was a call the Scriptures and the ethos of our church community wholeheartedly affirmed. But had Evon decided to continue with her law practice, it would have been no less a noble endeavor. Her gifts would simply be channeled to bring God's flourishing through a different field, as an extension of the work of our church.

One key question our church will ask our parishioners is, How can we get on God's agenda for your work in the world? This question in many ways casts our community in a different light. People realize that the church not only is sincerely curious, but also values their contribution both inside and outside of the church. Our parishioners are actively involved in the city, writing and rewriting stories through their presence at work. When they join God and church, their work becomes an extension of our mission in the world. With this posture our churches even become represented across different industries.

Whenever Joey, owner of Selah Bodyworks, a mobile massage company, sets up chairs in schools, corporate parties, and street festivals, his ministry and company by extension become the hands of God reaching out, providing health and mental wellness. Joey, through reflection and many conversations about the role of work and ministry, was able to make connections between God and his career. Whenever people's eyes open to this formative intersection, it becomes an indicator of spiritual growth. Seeing work through this prism allows people to see more Christ in more places, in some ways assuaging the guilt of not doing enough for Jesus.

Joey even invited a group of us over to one of his locations to pray over his establishment. In true charismatic form we prayed a blessing and laid hands on the different walls in the establishment. We prayed that everyone who would receive a massage there would receive the peace of Christ over their body and minds in a city that is captive to hurry and anxiety. These contextual prayers place the church within the intersections of a city where overwork and stress are commonplace.

PRACTICE: DISCERNING OUR COLLECTIVE RESPONSE

Discerning the nature of our contribution in a community at a particular moment is important. Our collective vocational discernment has thankfully come through the aid of many companions. One particular ally was our friend Richard Rivera. Richard is a native New Yorker and an organizational development consultant and facilitator. We call Rich the Yoda of facilitation in our circles. Richard facilitates groups like no other leader I've seen. Whether it's a corporate boardroom or a group of teachers in a conference room—two or two hundred people—he leads with the same mindful energy, forming seamless connections with his participants. Richard describes this kind of work as a means "to partner with God to change the world one room at a time." Our retreats together have helped us navigate questions and discern God's present plan for our community.

In many ways this discernment was the practice of a band of brothers found in the Old Testament called the Sons of Issachar, who were "200 chiefs, with all their relatives." All these men "understood the times and knew what Israel should do," a wisdom that worked concurrently with the movements of a specific time and place (1 Chronicles 12:32). Like them, we asked simple yet profound

questions such as "What time is it in the world today?" and
"What time is it for our church?" We took on a posture of openness
and attentiveness. We became more attuned to the intersection
of our gifts within our context, which grounded and defined our
collective work in our city.

When a building exploded in East Harlem at 9:31 a.m., March
12, 2014, several blocks away, we used Richard's wisdom for the
team and decided we would approach this crisis in prayer and
action. Our leadership met with Richard, gathering into a process
called "appreciate inquiry." We explored what our specific response to this crisis would be. Knowing our church had limited
resources, we were strategic. After some prayer and deliberation
we decided we could mobilize a network of churches, with our
church becoming a fiscal channel to provide financial resources
to First Spanish Church, which was once located in the building
that had exploded. Metro Hope Church became a hub for
churches seeking to provide First Spanish Church with resources
to replace what was lost.

Our vocation as a church can be grounded in collective responses similar to that of the Jewish exiles in the city of Babylon,
who were captive and in many ways disempowered. God would
provide them with a new impetus for living as exiles in Babylon,
instructing the exiles in the book of Jeremiah to

> build houses and settle down; plant gardens and eat what
> they produce. Marry and have sons and daughters; find
> wives for your sons and give your daughters in marriage,

so that they too may have sons and daughters. Increase in number there; do not decrease. Also, seek the peace and prosperity of the city to which I have carried you into exile. Pray to the Lord for it, because if it prospers, you too will prosper. (Jeremiah 29:5-7)

God's household rules could bless Babylon through Israel's daily distinctive, active, mindful living in the world. These instructions were in deep contrast to the separation from pagan nations God commanded earlier in Israel's history. In the Babylonian exile, the Israelites would now live as a cooperative within an empire community, being part of Babylon while honoring God's rule of the household as their first allegiance.

Today as we contemplate shalom in our own twenty-first century context, the church can encourage a form of responsive stewardship that takes into account not only personal budgets but also the larger economy it finds itself in.

BECOMING GOD'S CROWDSOURCE IN THE BARRIO

When churches help people reimagine how their gifts fit into God's greater economy, it reclaims a historical role for the church—a role both the Catholic and Eastern Orthodox churches have affirmed over the centuries, where the principle of economy is rendered in deeper and broader light.

While the term *economy* might conjure images of capitalism, NASDAQ, or even a bronze bull on a Wall Street sidewalk, the Greek word *oikonomia*, from which *economy* is derived, retains more robust significance and meaning. Oikonomia is defined as "the rule of the household," it also refers to "the responsibility given to humans in creation for managing the resources of the earth (Genesis 1:26). In the church, Christian stewardship involves the whole of life since all life comes from God and is to be lived for God's glory."

In God's "rule of the household," the church views its gifts and possessions as extensions of this household. People of Christ exercise their distinctive gifts within God's larger impetus for flourishing in the world.

At home we encourage our son to be a part of the oikonomia as a contributing member. Our daily practices involve love for neighbor, generosity, and hospitality for God's household translated into our zip code in Harlem. These gifts come in even the simple act of clearing the kitchen table on Taco Tuesday, or the way his artwork graces the front door greeting our neighbors and visitors.

If Christians realized they were an extension of God's greater household in the world, it would make a positive impact. Unfortunately, when many Christians move into a place it's a form of mindless living in the city, unconscious about the economic disparities and hardships of the surrounding neighborhood. The intention behind moving into a neighborhood can be for the simple reason that it is "up and coming," superseding any sense of awareness of neighborhood pain and suffering.

The recent boom in church plants in NYC has skewed toward middle-class models that favor the gentry and the elite in formerly working-class or middle-class neighborhoods. People bring in particular tastes, often overlooking the history and the particularity of long-established businesses, where market forces often favor the up and coming sensibilities. I've seen how our *panaderias* (local bakeries) have been making lattes (*café con leche*) for years, yet lack the local support of new tenants in the hood.

In my forty years in NYC, I've never witnessed a positive or just form of gentrification. In an often Darwinian housing and job market, it will inevitably favor the privileged. A recent article in the *New York Times* even highlighted how NYC Housing Authority residents in East Harlem feel like strangers in their own neighborhoods. Many East Harlemites find themselves moving to the surrounding boroughs, or Florida.

In our community the average median income for a household of four is less than $35,000, yet there are new luxury high rises being developed. Meanwhile 20 percent of New Yorkers put 50 percent of their income toward housing. These changes affect rent affordability for individuals and small local businesses alike. Our concern is the unraveling of the fabric of our neighborhood.

My wife and I have encouraged our church community to take mindful walks through their neighborhoods. Walking with Mayra, I find she will often stop at two or three businesses at a time, talking to local business owners like Maria, the young Mexican woman selling mango slices at the corner of 116th Street. Then we stop by the new cupcake place catering to Harlem's gentrifying palate. Mayra will take a menu, inquiring about how long they've been in business, promising to send people their way.

Within a three-mile radius in Harlem we personally know at least twenty business owners. This is no accident. We encourage our church to see local business support as a form of discipleship—a way of being present in neighborhoods with deep intention.

Our parishioners are reminded that every transaction is a way to keep resources flowing in a local community. And our leadership has bought into this mission wholeheartedly. Even to the point of enduring some bad start-up experiences. Like the time the new dental practice didn't use enough Novocain for John's fillings. I tried convincing him with a good pep talk: "If Jesus endured the cross, what's one dental procedure gone bad?"

He remained unconvinced.

I also share research on the "sticky effect" concerning the use of cash in a local establishment. Dollars used locally circulate in communities up to three times longer. Owners can then purchase from local suppliers, who pay local employees, who can then make purchases at the local market . . . and the gifts move on.

To contribute to economic flourishing is to "keep the gift moving," an insight from indigenous tribal wisdom. If our gifts stop, and we hoard (think Zacchaeus), or consistently reappropriate (shop elsewhere), imbalances will naturally occur. Notwithstanding, if middle- and upper-class people in poor neighborhoods support local business owners, local economies could function a lot differently.

In support of this idea NPR reported a study done by Network Science. The researchers tracked the shopping habits of 150,000 people in two major cities. Researchers concluded that if

5 percent of these consumers changed their shopping habits, a noticeable economic change could be seen in neighborhoods with fewer resources. The study states, "The addition of small changes in the shopping destinations of individuals can dramatically impact the spatial distribution of money flows in the city, and the frequency of encounters between residents of different neighborhoods."

What if churches supported these changes by encouraging not only parishioners but also neighborhood residents to buy local? This could have a quantifiable impact on a whole neighborhood economy. Yet there are even small steps churches can make to witness change on a local level.

As part of a sustained investment, our church supported the East Harlem Café. Our community and arts coordinator, Chantilly Mers, assisted Michelle, the café owner, in raising ten thousand dollars through an online campaign. The money went toward the purchase of a new refrigerator to provide customers with healthier eating options during a time when East Harlem was considered a food desert.

In continuing to sustain our engagement with East Harlem small businesses, our church also organizes monthly "cash mobs," mobilizing a group of community people to support local restaurants. Our first ever was at the East Harlem Café during a winter storm. Two of our church members volunteered as café servers to accommodate the crowd. Metro's worship band became the house band for the day. Our church and local residents packed out the café on one of the snowiest days of the

year. People from our local community board and local organizations were represented; it was successful particularly during
a long winter season with a low revenue tide. According to Michelle, the effort even assisted the café in meeting payroll for
that week.

We held another cash mob at a local apparel store named
Harlem Underground Clothing Company. The Sunday prior to
the event our church hosted the establishment owner. Charmaine had the opportunity to share her vision behind the
clothing store, which has been in existence since 1998 on Harlem's busiest corridor, a now-gentrifying shopping strip. The
next Sunday a group from our church shopped at the establishment after the service. We also invited neighborhood residents to attend. Charmaine reported that through our collective
efforts the store earned several times the revenue it had ever
made on any given Sunday, an economic boost for a clothing
store competing with big box stores less than a block away.

I would ponder afterward, What would happen if there was a
movement of churches in Harlem supporting locally owned
businesses in our community? How would the neighborhood
retain some of its local character, while the hopes and dreams,
even the personal economic vitality, of a neighborhood shop
owner become a priority to the church?

Not two weeks after our efforts, our church treasurer reported
that Harlem Underground Clothing Company tithed back to our
church. While this was never presented as a requirement for
our patronage, it was the embodiment of the ethic that the gift

(our resources) must keep moving. This is how neighborhood ecologies thrive and function, and what signs of economic shalom can look like in our local neighborhoods.

As churches we can harness the power of incarnational and mindful discipleship to become a vocational movement—a movement that shares Christ's concern for people's work in the world. A movement that reminds us that faith-filled work can be an adventure in our own backyard.

We can use our Sunday platforms to affirm entrepreneurs and workers we know personally in our community, and pray that as they prosper the neighborhoods would prosper as well. The church can be mindful in real time by creating liturgies to bless new start-ups in our church community and in our neighborhood. A church is never too small to support other start-ups; investing in smaller organizations provides an immediate and visible impact.

Developing this type of Christian consciousness will be a challenge for people whose consumer ethic has not been oriented by the good news of Christ, in a culture that is more oriented toward individualism. But to see oneself within the larger collective in God's oikonomia steers us into a particular kind of discipleship, replete with action that can reshape even our patterns and habits of consumption.

At each intersection of the neighborhood, there are formative questions—questions that can help orchestrate the medley of gifts and voices of God's priesthood of believers. How can our churches become present to these possibilities?

REFLECTION QUESTIONS

1. How can you use your gifts to be a blessing to people in the workplace?

2. What is the connection between your personal call and God's vision for the church? Your workplace? Your city? How can your agenda for work become more consciously and directly part of God's work in town? Country? City?

3. What steps can you take to become more mindful of your neighborhood history, culture, and economy?

4. What steps can you take to ensure your shopping patterns favor the local economy?

5. What can your church do to become more mindful of the local economy and its well-being?

7

STAYING TOGETHER
WHEN HOPE BECAME A HOUSEHOLD

Hospitality also requires letting go of one-dimensional concepts of people we don't know. As if this stranger were not a multi-faceted human being with a complex history, just as we know ourselves to be.

KATHLYN JAMES

Conducting our lives on a daily basis in close proximity to others guarantees that there will be tensions, misunderstandings, individual subjectivities, struggles and differences of opinion.

ARTHUR KATZ

A S SHE PACKED HER LUGGAGE we all felt a deep sense of loss. Sonya—an anchor resident of our intentional community, Hope House—was moving back home to

North Carolina. Sonya's mom was ill, and Sonya would move back down south to care for her and ensure she received the necessary supports.

Sonya was a matriarch in our church community. And like many pastors have known before me, when a church loses influential leadership, it has a way of unraveling some of the connective tissue that holds the family together. Sonya had become a common denominator in her open and willing presence, bringing together people that wouldn't ordinarily feel like they belonged.

Sonya's vulnerability was also a prism of sorts that allowed us to see others through her unsentimental, unconditional love. With a shepherding heart she individualized people—to the degree they might feel as if they were the only person that existed around her. Thankfully, in her being sent forth, Sonya left part of herself behind within the DNA of our church hospitality.

Church communities can never underestimate the power of the gifts of hospitality, fellowship, and proximity, nor overlook practitioners within the church who are stewards of such gravitational power. When people submit themselves, their hearts and homes and spaces for belonging together, the seeding of redemptive space is prepared for the gospel to flourish. Curtains are raised, and Christ is revealed—for momentary snapshots of what we have seen as "in Harlem as it is in heaven."

Time and proximity seem to be the ultimate commodities for this holy togetherness. Without time in both the momentous moments of life and the mundane moments, the ministry of racial justice in a crosscultural community will be limited in scope. When people commit to a particular form of staying together beyond being roommates or simply sharing space together, one can find a mystical staying power for the church, Christ's works rooted concretely in a neighborhood block.

Our church endeavored one day to take this discipleship challenge to the next level by forming an intentional community in East Harlem. Forming a ministry house for people to live the mission of Christ in a neighborhood meant three things: (1) the challenges of rooting church in a transient culture, (2) honoring some of the travails and messiness of life together in a diverse space, while (3) striving to find agreements that could be the fodder for growth together.

ROOTING HOPE IN A TRANSIENT CULTURE

The practice of staying in a transient and commitment-phobic culture with deep intention is a countercultural, courageous act. NYC is renowned for its frenetic pace, where invisible urgency takes residence in the air. Cars will zoom down a narrow street just to get to the red light, and a person rushing to buy milk at the local bodega can be easily mistaken for someone rushing to an emergency room. Indeed every place in the world has its modus operandi. And I've seen how NYC summons the inner thoroughbred in those who have migrated here from "slower" locations.

As my friends say, the hustle is real, and city culture can grate on most anyone swept up in that spirit. It's not uncommon for singles to live with up to four roommates in a shared living space to rustle up rent, while many married couples lack the luxury of a single-income partnership.

Our world here is craving quiet contemplative spaces where we can avoid being swept up in the real as well as false urgencies that exist. This requires a relational, contemplative theology connected to place and time, where staying put is more of a sacred calling than just a move into a preferred living space.

In *The Wisdom of Stability*, Jonathan Wilson-Hartgove writes, "Staying, we all know, is not the norm in our mobile culture. A great deal of money is spent each day to create desires in each of us that can never be fulfilled. I suspect that much of our restlessness is a return on this investment."

Restlessness is the unfortunate byproduct of rushing and mobility, as well as a major impediment to transformation. Those who have come centuries before us in places such as North Africa, the desert mothers and fathers, the mystics, have attested to how growth comes when we slow down and dwell in God's presence. The end result will be not just about missional accomplishment, but flourishing in communion with God and others.

Time and place are valuable commodities for our being forged together in community. Consequently, churches cannot reduce dismantling racial barriers to a workshop or a conference. Implicit bias about women, communities, people, and places will not be challenged without an immersion that allows people to soak in an environment in close proximity to others, with the resources of the faith.

Growth in Christ can be slow and happens best in the ecology of a community. Jesus infuses our growth through a holy tethering when he says, "I am the vine; you are the branches.... Apart from me you can do nothing" (John 15:5). Scripture attests that our staying connected to Christ within the context of community produces enduring fruit—the capacity to love well in healthy proximity to God and others.

Christ's use of the vine metaphor also points to nourishment in relationship by way of sustained connectivity. "Apart from me you can do anything" is a bold, eternity-laced declaration about the nature of our connection. Christ is the life source that mediates relationship, otherwise known as a "Love Supreme." Christ, whose very identity is community through the Trinitarian dance of Father, Son, and Holy Spirit, invites us into deep, intentional community.

Jesus further speaks about the substance of relational faith:

As the Father has loved me, so have I loved you. Now remain in my love. If you keep my commands, you will remain in my love, just as I have kept my Father's commands and remain in his love. I have told you this so that my joy may be in you and that your joy may be complete. My command is this: Love each other as I have loved you. Greater love has no one than this: to lay down one's life for one's friends. (John 15:9-13)

Flourishing through love takes place when disciples remain in a web of relationship facilitated and joyfully nourished by God. At its best this will debunk any form of information-driven discipleship. In fact, through Christ's approach, deep orthodoxy (right thinking) is expressed in a deep relational orthopraxy (right doing). The very content of our theological thinking and our actions will be in connection with God through others, and with others through God. This leads us to arrange our lives around dwelling with Christ, while seeking belonging in one another.

Dwelling with God and people through Christ prevents spiritual growth from becoming disembodied and even disembedded from a place in time. For to be a follower of Jesus Christ in its very essence is a communitarian practice. Each interaction, each conversation we have with other sisters and brothers is an opportunity to get to know Christ all the more.

Our decision to abide with Christ and people in space and time is the first crucial practice of our development. The next step in staying together is defining what the rhythms of staying look like in a specific context. Our church leadership took on this task of discerning how to "enflesh" our core value of deep community by way of the intentional community movement.

HOPE HOUSE: MOMENTS, PLACE, AND RECONCILIATION

Our endeavor toward intentional community was connected to a long tradition within Christian history dating back to the monastic movements of Northern Africa. Over time certain religious orders would follow these patterns and establish them throughout Europe, in many instances practicing a *rule of life* governing their rhythms together as a community.

A more recent example is Koinonia Farms in Georgia, a diverse community that came together in 1942 over farming, racial equality, and housing development, which eventually evolved into what we know today as Habitat for Humanity International.

For our church, building community has been a core value since inception. We have encouraged people in our church to move into close proximity with one another as an expression of lived mission. Seeking to live out this value led us to the formation of an intentional community, an experiment and adventure that came together rather suddenly one hot July summer day.

One day some of us were helping the Cid family, who were longtime members of Metro Hope Church, to whack weeds in the backyard of their townhouse in East Harlem. It was 90 degrees, just before the height of the noonday sun. Right away our lack of a green thumb was exposed. After working up a good sweat, a couple of us made our way down to the lower level of the Cids' house for refreshments.

Andy, John, and I saw a large, empty, finished basement, and three bedrooms available above. The space communicated coziness and welcome. Imaginations were sparked about how the space could be repurposed for the church to develop more of a presence in our community. Alfredo and Yudy Cid would join this radical vision as well. Renting apartments in their townhouse below market rate in our gentrifying neighborhood, they were committed to helping people stay in the neighborhood.

Our church envisioned Hope House as an exercise in radical community. Being roommates in an apartment was one thing; "life together" was another matter altogether. Life together communicated a deeper sense of shared experience, sharing a mission on a block. I find moments of decision like this present themselves few and far between—invitations to leave the safety and security of one's home and venture into a "strange" land (or space) in order to live as a new community of Christ. Whenever people are willing and ready to give themselves wholeheartedly to an invitation and calling, asking for less than people's lives isn't worthy of the call. Christ's call is sacrificial, is life altering, and truly raises the stakes of faith.

Pursuing deep fellowship takes a compelling invitation, joining God and God's diverse family in shared place and mission together. William Jennings presents a vision for such a space when he writes, "Imagine a people defined by their cultural differences yet who turn their histories and cultural logics toward a new determination, a new social performance of identity. . . . Thus the words and ways of one people join those of another, and another, each born anew in community seeking to love and honor those in its midst."

Our first iteration of Hope House immersed us in our neighborhood as a concrete expression of incarnational ministry. Proximity would foster spontaneous moments together with our neighbors. From these conversations, current news about the block would arrive. One of our consistent conversation topics was the corner grill/deli/bodega/café, which was having some identity issues in our gentrifying neighborhood. We were also prayerfully concerned about the lack of foot traffic on that corner of Park Avenue. This insight would be one of our early awakenings to support small businesses, and even to take it a step further by introducing ourselves to the owner.

At Hope House we saw glimpses of our working toward a rootedness and communal belonging. We planted a garden, raising resources through the church in the process. A good majority of the church was involved in everything from hauling dirt to dedicating the garden space in prayer. Rachael, one of our house members, would plant, care for, and harvest the garden, and we shared the produce with our church folks on Sunday. It was a way to connect the fruit of the church's prayers for the house with the fruit of the labor put into the garden. There were many afternoons when I would sit in the quiet of the garden, and for certain moments, it was otherworldly. That is, until the rumble of the Metro North Train rudely brought me back to the block.

About one year into the life of Hope House we organized a street festival, inviting local artists and small business owners we had come to know, as well as nonprofits and neighbors, to name a few. We had an intergenerational drummers' circle in keeping with the tradition of drumming performed at Marcus Garvey Park. And while we received some pushback from a neighbor or two concerned about damage to their property due to our event, we otherwise would become seamlessly connected with our community.

I found the more challenging aspects of community would come in the day-to-day living negotiations, not so much the engagement with surrounding neighbors. In this space we weren't just grappling with the complexities of squaring away personality differences, but also working through real differences in culture and race in our quest for deeper belonging.

STAYING TOGETHER THROUGH RACIAL
TENSIONS IN SPACE MAKING

The Cid family had been generous with their home in East Harlem. Alfredo Cid grew up in the Dominican Republic as one of ten children. Hence, the idea of this sort of proximity was nostalgic and familiar in some ways—Alfredo brought first-generation Latino sensibilities of *familismo* into the negotiation of space. Other members had a different interpretation of how space was to be negotiated, seeing space as less "enmeshed" and more with clearly defined boundaries. Through imperfect and intense negotiations about space we were able to divvy the house into common areas, as well as honor the personal space of each house member.

Interestingly, the most formative dimensions of our being together were not just in routine prayer times, meals, or any other form of gathering. Rather, it was in the negotiation of space and living habits, traversing the "in betweens" of community life, where I sensed growth happened the most. We found that these processes could either break us down or bring us closer together, depending on how forthright we were with our communication.

Add racial differences to this and it took on another level of energy and vulnerability.

In our first iteration of Hope House, Sonya lived with Andy, who had lived in Brussels and East Harlem prior to joining our church, and John, who had lived north of Harlem in Washington Heights for over seven years. Each one of them is simply a remarkable person.

John has an amazing way of bringing people together with levity, with a real heart to see racial barriers broken down. Andy is the son of a theology professor. He has one of the most generous spirits of anyone I know. He also brought a very particular perspective as someone from overseas—he was continually encouraging the work we were doing, since he hadn't witnessed many efforts like it led by people of color.

Sonya, an African American woman from the South, embodied genuine Southern charm and hospitality. When she agreed to be in sustained proximity to two white brothers in Andy and John, though, she could not have been prepared for what the experience could conjure in her. Everything, including how space was lived in, arranged, and cleaned, was not minutia, but elemental for negotiating and sustaining relationships.

Space and place can be an extension of a person's culture and heritage. Whenever space is somehow violated, it can be experienced as a violation of one's personhood. This happens regardless of race, and yet race and gender can add another dimension of complexity in the negotiation of space. When space is shared, it can bring up all kinds of issues from deep within, and tensions common in any living situation can become more pronounced in a crosscultural dynamic. Sonya and John shared with me openly about how proximity allowed for exercises in both vulnerability and courage.

Sonya didn't realize at the time how cultural differences would come into play during particular encounters. For a time while living at Hope House she was underemployed—and as a result she could feel vulnerable as a contributing member of the household. She discerned how these instances could make the most casual interactions laden with emotional triggers.

One day Sonya hosted me, John, and Andy for coffee at Hope House's kitchen island area. Sonya would later recount how serving me coffee as a typical gesture of hospitality felt natural. On the other hand, when she served John and Andy, something welled up within her as an African American woman. (I would emphasize *woman* as I realize there was also a gender dynamic that I have too easily overlooked in the past.) Sonya shared with me how serving them had conjured up images of black women and servitude in the South—the feeling of being seen as a mammy. A coffee moment over a kitchen island became a personal fissure tethered to our country's racial fault line.

Rhythms of life together can home in on the traumas and hurts that we collectively carry. And those who are in proximity to one another have the shared burden of holding space and pain together in trust. Spaces that allow for these raw, unvarnished moments can be healing and redemptive—taking the pain that comes from a broken world and providing people a healing balm by way of safety and embrace.

Through processing this moment over time, Sonya would later recall all of the "spiritual capital" the three had already cultivated as a new community. The holidays they spent together; the authentic conversations on race, where both Andy and John would take on the posture of learners; barbecues together with the larger family; and the shared responsibility in the house of hosting the church. Sonya mentioned that they were all "plugged in" because of an impetus to dialogue, refusing to shrink away from arduous spaces.

The biggest lesson she would relate during her moments of intentional community is how her idea of community had been usurped by something redemptive. In Sonya's own words:

> What helped me through this experience was remembering the moments with them. All the times we came together and cleaned together. . . . Unbeknownst to me, we had been stitching the fabric of community all along. All the times we hosted, I didn't feel that we were strangers, but family preparing for more family. These memories—in the midst of the difficult moments—allowed me to transcend, and it provided me healing about my perspective about community. It gave me a new hope for community. Joining together added substance to community. That reality added far more than what I could've imagined.

Everyone should have a Hope House experience. If for no other reason than to lead a more Christlike life, our personal experiences in community can have a positive public consequence. We take what we learn in community and bring it into the world.

A community's mission to stay put together in Christ can catalyze a community to be of public good as a witness to the world: "By this everyone will know that you are my disciples, if you love one another" (John 13:35). Love is consistently seeking to understand the other in a spirit of humility bound up in grace.

From this vantage point, John relates,

> As a white male I usually have the privilege of dealing with and confronting racism when and how I choose. Avoidance is almost always an option. But living in Hope House in close proximity to a woman of color made it very difficult to avoid it altogether. . . . [My] white world got smaller.

John further described how allowing Sonya into his life was formative in helping him work out some of his "deep seated white prejudices." He recognized how racism cannot be worked out as a white person without close proximity to persons of color. John learned how community was a necessity this way. He adds,

> My journey with Sonya and Andy at Hope House wasn't full of earth-shattering epiphanies. It was more like a steady, unrelenting river that carves a new landscape through solid rock. It was through an accumulation of difficult conversations, mundane life moments, and laughter that my perspective was forever altered.

Spiritual transformation of this kind does not happen without rootedness, proximity, and time. Discipleship in a transient culture like NYC, or in a world where our attention spans are captive to a multiplicity of distractions, will require a covenant, a form of agreement, to stay in places and moments with a contemplative mindset.

ALMOST COVENANT AND THE NEED FOR AGREEMENTS

One of my most vital lessons in creating intentional community is that blessed togetherness will not be sustained without clarity and agreements. God is a God of covenant and law; God's wisdom shows in lovingly fostering the boundaries of relationships to create conditions of shalom. Covenants and agreements are not just contractual but rooted in arranging life together around mutual gift giving—the promise each community member makes to render what God has given them to contribute, an aspect of covenant often overlooked. This final section shows where some of my lack of attention to detail in this area could have made things more difficult. I don't so much lament our collective mistakes but reflect on the courage to grow through them, rooted in the hope of seeing God's grace work through healthy incarnational communities.

By studying and yet somehow overlooking some of how monastic traditions are arranged, I bypassed an important step in the staying together process: how intentional communities are safeguarded with a written "way of life." Hope House could've integrated a more formal framework to guide relationships, with an orientation and "onboarding" process for new arrivals to the house. In doing so, perhaps in a retreat space, we could've provided an opportunity for house residents to be infused with our collective vision for dwelling together. Conceivably it could have been instituted as an annual practice—orienting people not only to welcome them, but also to get them acclimated to the norms, culture, and rules of the community. Covenants can protect against ambiguity of expectations, which can place undue pressure on members to figure things out too often.

In her book *Covenant and Commonwealth*, Marcia Pally describes covenant as being a

> relationship of reciprocal concern, the commitment by each to give for the flourishing of the other, generously, not quid pro quo. It is a form of relationship in which each party is distinct and through which each becomes more of the distinct person she is. The gift of commitment—of having one's needs and concerns taken as consideration-worthy—is how distinct persons flourish whether in childhood or business [or in church].

Pally's framework for covenant here can produce both short-term and long-term agreements. In other words, intention and mutuality can be guided through agreements, taking into consideration how "each party is distinct," which also means that covenant can facilitate a mutuality in honoring one another.

Relationships rooted in covenant agreements present the gifts to be exchanged and boundaries to be observed in writing for the flourishing, and ultimately the protection, of relationships. Devoting time to write clear and formal covenant agreements that would govern life—from times of sabbath, rent payments, space usage, time together, time apart, and Enneagram profiles, to participation in the life of the neighborhood, to name a few—was vital.

Covenant can serve as a trellis to support relational growth and ought to precede any moves into sustained proximity and presence. If not, intentional community can fall victim to the complexities of informality, where too much ambiguity can lead to feelings of instability. When people feel a sense of instability, it's natural for trust in leadership to wane. Inevitably any agreements fostered through the bonds of informality can fall victim to relational strain. Too much informality grates on relationships and can drain away the joy of mission together.

Tom Rath, author of *Strengths Based Leadership*, describes how leaders can foster healthy climates by way of four factors: trust, stability, compassion, and hope. The first, trust, is vital—without it the other three aspects become less plausible. Trust happens when leaders are true to their word, while also cultivating a stability that comes with honest and clear communication.

When I wanted to avoid too much conflict about landlord negotiations or space considerations, I over-relied on wit, friendliness, and the history of friendship to make agreements on some matters. Without an agreement I found the stability that community members needed could be lacking. For example, it wasn't fair for matters related to rent, space, and so on to be left up in the air for long stretches of time.

My leadership philosophy for the life of the house was based on leading through the strength of relationships. This worked until it didn't. I underestimated the strain that life and ministry in the city would have on me and the house members. Having been overwhelmed with concerns about church sustainability while shepherding both a church and a house, I can now see the wisdom in having a minister just for the intentional community.

A small church like ours pulled the members of the house to also work in the church. Those living in Hope House felt a great enmeshment with the church that was overwhelming at times. We could have better structured and honored a more appropriate distance between house and church.

One of our house members, Jacob, was part of our church worship band, worked full time, was in seminary (in a dual degree program), and managed responsibilities in the mission of the house. This kind of mixing of different responsibilities is the norm more than the exception in NYC. I often wonder whether the mission of the house could've focused more on sabbath and rest. A countercultural covenant could resist compounding how the powers and principalities of our culture contribute to hurry, stress, and burnout.

Our Hope House community would witness five fruitful years, and the building would be used as an office space for several more after. Today I still believe in the power of intentional communities and know that if planted strategically, these community expressions can possibly have more impact on a neighborhood than a church disinterested in its local context.

Every now and again I peer out of my window down the block to the Hope House backyard, fond of our beautiful memories and relationships that endure until this day. I also remain staunchly hopeful about the transformative power of people who show up together—dwelling purposely in one small corner of the block, witnessing God's love perform miracles through covenant community.

REFLECTION QUESTIONS

1. What are your personal challenges to sustaining deep relationships in a church fellowship?

2. How might our surroundings and culture, stage of life, or lifestyle rail against our commitment to deeper fellowship?

3. When you "do" community with other people, how is that time spent together? What's happening?

4. What formal agreements can be made between you and others—for a period of time—to enter into deeper, Christ-centered fellowship? How can the church support this venture?

5. How might the truth of God being a community—Three in One—possibly shape your view of independence?

6. What opportunities might you have for moving into proximity to mission together?

PART 3

SEE

8

LOOK AGAIN
GENEROUS SEEING AS A MEASURE OF DISCIPLESHIP

American privilege, is blurring my
vision, inherited sickness.

ALLEN STONE, "AMERICAN PRIVILEGE"

I am an invisible man. No, I am not a spook like
those who haunted Edgar Allan Poe: Nor am I one
of your Hollywood movie ectoplasms. I am a man
of substance, of flesh and bone, fiber and liquids—
and I might even be said to possess a mind. I am
invisible, simply because people refuse to see me.

RALPH ELLISON, *INVISIBLE MAN*

Love casts out fear, but we have to get over the
fear in order to get close enough to love them.

**DOROTHY DAY, "IN PEACE IS MY
BITTERNESS MOST BITTER"**

I N 2015 BARNA CONDUCTED A STUDY in partnership with a parachurch organization called the Navigators on "the state of discipleship." Barna's findings, I found, can inspire some great conversation about discipleship in our larger North American context, as the study covered a range of topics, including disparities between what church leaders and church attenders see as spiritual growth.

Barna's research used a comparison group that included practicing Christians, nonpracticing Christians, and Navigator alumni. According to the study, only 1 percent of church leaders say, "Today's churches are doing very well at discipling new and young believers." In contrast, 52 percent of church attenders (people who had attended church in the past six months at least once per month) thought their churches were doing a good job of "helping people grow spiritually."

For many church leaders, the disparities between what we think and what our parishioners think can keep us up at night. What we believe about Christian habits of formation can be disparate from our parishioners' sensibilities, making the shape of discipleship a challenge of expectations.

If we can all agree—at the risk of sounding simplistic—that our end result is to see people become more Christlike, then we have a good starting point for this discussion. Yet further discussion is warranted lest we fail to even determine what we mean when we say "Christlike." Barna's research affirms that people's view of being Christlike can entail "using the way of Jesus as a means of pursuing the way of self."

In contrast Christ's life demonstrates how genuine concern for others is at the heart of Christian maturity. This can extricate evangelicalism from an overindulgent concern with the self. Discipleship can then become more dimensional through stark reminders and prophetic voices posing a sincere challenge on how "life's most persistent and urgent question is, 'What are you doing for others?'"

Beneath the surface of Dr. King's prophetic question also emerges a pastoral task, a parallel challenge to profoundly awaken the heart of our Christian formation. Namely, how do we even perceive those we are called to serve and love? How does my growth and personal devotion to Christ translate into me seeing diverse others with the eyes of Christ? After all, how we see and perceive a person is just as important as how we serve them.

The fear of many pastors across the spectrum of Christian faith is a discipleship that misses the deep priorities and practices of Christ and the Scriptures. This is where the Bible points us in the true direction of measuring spiritual growth.

A DISCIPLESHIP MEASURE: SEEING LIKE CHRIST

Some of Christ's most spirited encounters with religious leaders were about how Jewish law was to be seen and interpreted in a social context. Jesus would confront religious leaders who, in terms of the law, were knowledgeable yet somehow blind to its essence—the inherent good news about God's love for the whole world. Many were challenged around their social imagination for compassion and inclusivity, blinding them to Christ and the work that Christ did through others.

In Luke chapter 7, Jesus' encounter with Simon over dinner was all about a new way of seeing someone. As Jesus ate as a guest in Simon's home, a woman showed up uninvited and began to wash Jesus' feet with her tears. Consistent with Middle Eastern practice, Jesus would have most likely been reclining at the table, locating this woman in extreme proximity to Jesus.

Simon, seeing this happening in his own home, said, "If this man were a prophet, he would know who is touching him and what kind of woman she is—that she is a sinner" (Luke 7:39). Simon's critique brought Jesus' prophetic bonafides into question. Were not prophets seers? Those who supposedly had divine insight into things?

But Jesus would divert attention away from himself, in no way attempting to prove himself or his actions as a recipient of this woman's gift. Somehow, all in one instance, Jesus offered not only a question but also an interruption, placed at the right time to bend the arc of the conversation back to what matters most.

"Simon, do you see this woman?"

Jesus' question made this woman the highlight of the moment, pointing Simon back to her, vulnerable in her courageousness yet invisible to him and to many—even to the point of being nameless in a Scripture text.

"Simon, do you see this woman?" was a loaded and rich question for Simon's consideration. The word *see* in this context goes beyond a simple, "Hey Simon, come take a look." Actually, put another way, it could be, "Simon do you perceive? Contemplate? Discern this person in front of you?"

Contemplative sight—seeing others together with Jesus—will challenge us to see others in fuller dimension. With Christ's Spirit providing us a divine lens, we can behold people in a fuller humanity as image bearers of Christ. This is what the Bible and the church for centuries have deemed as revelation.

The moment Simon said, "what kind of woman," he would deny the image of God in her, endorsing her invisibility. Simon's reductionist seeing could not locate this woman as a child whose sins could be forgiven. He would trap her both in her gendered body and in her neighborhood reputation.

What does Jesus do as an exercise in revelation? He asks Simon to look again.

Jesus' question would challenge (even perhaps haunt) Simon and provide an opportunity to add dimension to Simon's myopic sight. In one fell swoop, Jesus elevated this woman, demonstrating how one of her greater virtues was her own sight. She saw the greatest love reclining before her, a love and grace overlooked by many in the religious community.

> Do you see this woman? I came into your house. You did not give me any water for my feet, but she wet my feet with her tears and wiped them with her hair. You did not give me a kiss, but this woman, from the time I entered, has not stopped kissing my feet. You did not put oil on my head,

but she has poured perfume on my feet. Therefore, I tell you, her many sins have been forgiven—as her great love has shown. But whoever has been forgiven little loves little. (Luke 7:44-47)

To see our common humanity wrapped up with others in our brokenness and in our beauty, in our sinfulness as people who need forgiveness, and in our places as saints, children of the Most High, is to see a fuller narrative of redemption.

Jesus' question should challenge any of us at any given table in our world. In our current day, women find themselves uninvited to many tables, reduced as image bearers by our world to a level beneath what God intended. An exercise in holy sight makes it imperative for men to continue to see, affirm, and honor the image of God in women in the world.

In a 2016 TED talk, Jimmy Carter said, "The number one abuse of human rights on earth . . . is the abuse of women and girls." Meanwhile a recent statistic by Human Rights First states that 71 percent of trafficking victims around the world are women and girls. This becomes locally evident in parts of New York City where massage parlors outnumber Starbucks coffee places. While women are expected to be advocates for other women, how powerful is it when men speak up as well? Men can rise up, divest themselves of privilege, and combat a cultural logic that can often reduce woman to objects. Altogether it is a deeply spiritual matter in a world where #MeToo has become a common lament.

Seeing others as Jesus does is a true discipleship metric with massive cultural and social implications. Part of developing a contemplative form of seeing is considering the people we encounter differently. In the next sections I will describe three practices followers of Christ can consider as we together look again with Christ.

PRACTICE 1—HONORING PEOPLE: WEIGHTY SIGHT

To honor people is to behold them in more substantial ways. When God commands the people of Israel to honor their parents in the book Exodus, the mandate assigns significant value to those who brought them into the world. The word *honor* in the Hebrew is consistent with this imperative, as one definition of honor is "to make heavy." In other words God was pressing on the people of Israel not to take this relationship lightly.

Honoring in practice evolves over time, because the way people essentially see their parents can grow. Maturity might dictate that we see our parents differently than when we were, say, children or adolescents. Growing up there were many aspects to our parents that remained invisible to us. But in honoring, adding weight to their value, spending time listening to repeated stories, we might actually grow to see our parents as whole worlds, reaching out, with trajectories, living through the seasons of life, working through feelings, dreams, and aspirations. We might grow to see our parents (or elders) for everything they are and aspire to be—in all of their light, love, and fragility. Our parents eventually would become human to us—do you remember that epoch-making moment when you first realized this?

They actually have sex.

Their feelings can be hurt.

They live with regrets and disappointments and dreams unfulfilled.

Certain relationships can conceivably remind us it is possible to encounter others with a renewed posture of discovery. In this discovery we will find that family, even strangers, can become more human as image bearers in the world. Now what if we took this same Old Testament ethic and applied it to the church family? The human family? The act of honoring can change the posture of relationships, creating a new inquisitiveness about others. We won't honor what we are uninterested in. But if we become proximate with curious intention, it opens up avenues for seeing things we overlooked, even stereotyped at one juncture.

Honoring can traverse all forms of relationship. I once uncovered my own narrow sight, my own myopic view of ministry regarding rural areas when working with a seminary intern named Robert Russo. Robert had worked as an organizer against mountaintop mining in a town in Appalachia. Together we became co-learners here in East Harlem through numerous conversations. Robert pointed out how poor people in rural areas are often caricatured by both the media and urban dwellers. In turn, we taught him about poverty in the barrio and the anxiety created in our communities of color by racial profiling by the police. From that moment forward our stories carried more weight and sanctity through empathic listening. We would now witness the worlds we both represented with much more proportion and magnitude.

Robert even helped some of us city dwellers plant a garden in East Harlem. Through planting together, sharing laughs, and telling stories, many of us developed a new perspective on rural poverty, and Robert learned what poverty looks like in a gentrifying Harlem. Our conversations also taught me how poverty does not discriminate based on location. When Jesus said, "Blessed are the poor," he didn't just mean urban poor or town and country poor. He meant *the* poor.

This mutual honoring, an ascribing of value and weight, came with time and relationship. People and places can reflect God's image; therefore, to dismiss any of these is to dishonor the image of God. What if the church began to enter and honor these places of disinheritance and disavowal? What if we had substantive conversations with others in a spirit of honoring their realities?

We need the Spirit's help for a more ripened curiosity concerning those we overlook or stereotype and fail to love well. How are we honoring whole communities that show up in reductionist headlines? Christ would beckon us to look again, even exchange our lesser questions for deeper questions about others.

PRACTICE 2—HONORING THROUGH BETTER INQUIRY: SACRED CURIOSITY

Crafting questions in a spirit of genuine curiosity and concern for those we've overlooked is an act of love. Our world would be a more whole place if we began to teach our children to contemplate people with sacred curiosity, at least in the way we contemplate a good poem, song, or painting at a museum. To merely look at a painting once might be to miss the deeper message the art carries. To speed through lines of poetry is to miss the mystery that beckons us to look again.

Inquiring about how to better love others is to pursue others for simply being God's workmanship. Surely this is a contemplative act as much as it is a conversational one. Maintaining prayerful curiosity about others in a divided world can reshape our minds, transforming the stale images and experiences of certain people groups, and cause an upheaval in our memory banks, propelling us in the direction of better questions about people.

More specifically, how do our questions honor communities when they face pain and tragedy? I wonder at times—even years later—how more generous seeing would have altered the national conversation after the death of Michael Brown or Eric Garner at the hands of police.

Our country has not historically honored the image of God in black people. We don't value black lives as image bearers in the same way we do the rest of the world. As a pastor friend, Efrem Smith, once tweeted, "All lives matter equally to God. But in this upside down, broken and bizarro world, not all lives are treated equally."

Today's conversation can very much resemble Jesus' conversation with the teacher of the law in the parable of the good

Samaritan (Luke 10:25-37). In the teacher's attempt to differentiate who was the right neighbor to help, he narrowed down the scope of compassion for some versus others. Jesus responded with his own question: "Who was the neighbor to the man in need?" At that moment Jesus had the teacher contemplate his response while engaging a lifeless body on the Jericho road, grounding "neighboring" through seeing and acting with eyes of compassion.

How might our very questions delay love and compassion in a moment when it is needed most? With police brutality a prevalent issue in communities of color, the church's response to suffering and trauma has been limited or misappropriated at times. One only needs to read the comment threads in certain forums and see that Christians' views have been co-opted, commonly sounding like an echo of media sound bites.

How we engage both personal and social suffering in the world is a conscious or unconscious response to particular questions. Some questions about social events can potentially invite us into deeper fellowship with others, and some questions can cause us to be distant from the heart of suffering.

In the Scriptures, Jesus could take people's lesser questions and reframe them, transforming the terms and agreements for more fruitful conversation. Followers of Christ are also called to enter into methods of alternative inquiry. Today if we take Christ's approach, we engage a matter potentially fraught with blaming a certain individual, or fixated on the facts of a case, and rescript it as an exercise in helping others to see with compassion.

We are, after all, the church, not the court of law. Each one individually has a role.

Both inside and outside the church many questions about race derive from sincere curiosity, from people looking to learn more. One question I've received was, "Why can't everyone just have the mindset that everyone is different, and that just because people are of a certain race it doesn't mean they're all the same?" Reframing the question, I asked, "What are the factors that contribute to creating a mindset where difference isn't embraced?" We live in a world that creates cultures and mindsets. Therefore prayerful questions can allow us to see with clarity and depth the deeply rooted issues at work.

Another popular question I get from many white people about police encounters with black and brown people is, "Why can't black and brown people just listen to the police?" Understanding the sentiment, I then ask, reframing the question: "What is happening in communities of color to cause an overall distrust with community policing? How can unconscious bias lead police to overexert authority in an encounter with a black or brown individual?"

Having people reflect on the basis of their biases through reflective questions can become a form of conversational spiritual formation, of seeing the image of God more fully through inquiry. A good question can pry open the singular narratives and stereotypes people have adopted about others.

PRACTICE 3—HONORING STORIES:
SEEING WITH GENEROUS EYES

Novelist Chimamanda Ngochi Adichie once gave a TED talk called "The Danger of a Single Story." She described the effects of reducing others, even whole countries, to a one-dimensional narrative, creating caricatures that are reinforced over time. Ultimately it is a limited, even stingy way of seeing people.

Scripture makes a connection between our eyes and our generosity when Jesus says, "The eye is the lamp of the body. If your eyes are healthy, your whole body will be full of light" (Matthew 6:22). Some scholars believe this enigmatic text is best seen through the eyes of Hebraic idiom—both the Midrash and our holy Scriptures reference a good eye as a generous eye.

In the Old Testament there are references to "bountiful eyes" and eyes that "look grudgingly on the poor." Having a good eye is consistently related to stewarding our lives in an outward fashion, on behalf of others, against a misappropriated love of worldly possessions. What our eyes treasure can become a reflection of our heart.

In *Jesus the Jewish Theologian*, Brad Young writes, "The generous person with a 'good eye' is driven by a concern to help others and to see their needs met. The selfish person is consumed by one interest: what belongs to him or her." Generous eyes allow us to look outward, look again at what we might have missed the first time. We can begin to ask ourselves how our vista might lack generosity when it comes to sharing our belongings, our space, our time, our eyes and ears. One might find that this can be experienced only in proximity to stories. Listening to others' stories has a way of encouraging us to possibly see more generously.

During the summer of 2016 my sight became a little less stingy through my facilitation work with people who were formerly incarcerated with organizations like Exodus Transitional Community and Community Connections for Youth (CCFY). I cofacilitated a training with my colleague and mentor Rev. Alfonso Wyatt. For decades Rev. Wyatt lived with the most generous eyes I've ever witnessed, mindfully working with young people of color, who are often rendered invisible by societies' single stories. Our training goal was to provide support to youth mentors, the majority of whom had returned home from prison.

Together we facilitated topics around strengths-based leadership, emotional health, and facing the hidden shadows and traumas of our lives. At one session the mentors would have an opportunity to share their stories. I didn't realize it at the time, but I unconsciously thought each story would be similar to the next. My outlook was not as generous as I thought it would be.

Reverend and I sat through narratives of pain and resilience. Each story was beautifully and vulnerably told with graceful nuance. Each shared how redemption was found even through the mistakes they had made. Life for some had provided them wisdom deeper and more generous beyond the life of crime.

One young man named Jamel shared about his first drug deal in the lobby of a Brooklyn housing development. On this day he would reach for his stash to attempt his first sale. As he extended his hand to a certain woman buyer, he had the stunning realization that he had handed the drugs to his best friend's mother. Jamel's gaze would meet this familiar face knowing full well in that instant that dealing drugs was not for him. He had seen more than just a drug user; he had seen family. Only years later—after being incarcerated—would he realize how his dealing was connected to a larger story, a more human story, of how he, his best friend's mother, and his neighbors were all part of a larger hood household. Jamel now sees everyone in his community as his best friend's mother—bearers of God's image. His eyes have only become more generous.

My own eyes were opened to the way the criminal justice system can reduce people to a single story of punishment. These returning citizens are worlds unto themselves, reaching out to others, capable of rescripting narratives, transforming lives, and mentoring others down the same path. Ultimately because of their sacrifice in transforming the lives of young people through mentoring, they have earned the right to be called credible messengers. This is a community with more resilience than most of us would ever fathom.

Today I have the privilege of facilitating these same trainings with Jamel as he inspires and supports others returning from prison. Jamel and I have also teamed up to lead pilgrimages with churches and faith-based organizations about a faith response to criminal justice in East Harlem. During our time we encourage people to see beyond a single story and to see people in prisons with more generosity—or, put another way, to be more Christlike.

Churches that see with the eyes of Christ are churches that have been trained to look again. Though there may be much suffering, beauty, and redemption in our own pews and provinces that we have perhaps overlooked, a formation that contemplates others as God's workmanship, that asks better questions and sees more broadly because of the importance of people's stories, can remove the scales, freeing people out of spiritual blindness.

REFLECTION QUESTIONS

1. How was being "Christlike" defined in your home or church context?

2. How do Christ's lenses challenge cultural norms that reinforce sexism, invisibility, and the "bro codes" of our day?

3. What assumptions and questions do you need to reexamine that might shape limited views about people of another culture? What questions can you begin to craft in sacred curiosity about another cultural group?

4. What are ways you can begin to honor—ascribe "weight" to—other people in other places?

5. What are ways we've given in to the "single story" when it comes to certain people groups?

6. How can our churches correct the misguided narratives our world has adopted about marginalized communities in society? What role can Sunday service play in this movement?

9

CURATING HEAVEN
KNOWING GOD THROUGH DANCE AND DIRGE

Earth's crammed with heaven,
And every common bush afire with God.

ELIZABETH BARRETT BROWNING

That I may know Him and the power of His
resurrection and the fellowship of His sufferings.

PHILIPPIANS 3:10 NASB

W E ARE A CULTURE fascinated with memes. Memes
are those captioned images or videos we often see in
our social network feeds. They can capture an idea or a collective
sentiment, and they have a great way of interpreting specific
moments. In a *meh* kind of culture, these symbols can humor-
ously, even prophetically, point the church into some deeper
truths about the world we live in, in light of some of our
great divisions.

Some of us might remember Olympic medalist McKayla Maroney back in the 2012 Summer Olympics. McKayla was favored to win the individual women's vault final. On this day, though, McKayla would slip during her vault routine, resulting in silver instead. During the medal ceremony, an image captured McKayla for a very brief moment while her lips were pursed to the left and her arms were folded, body language that perhaps betrayed some disappointment.

The internet would run with this image, morphing it into a meme with the caption "McKayla's not impressed." McKayla's image became an internet sensation and would be superimposed onto many other scenarios. McKayla meets Obama—she's not impressed. Space mission to Mars—McKayla's not impressed. McKayla received all this attention in good humor, even posing with the president during a visit to the White House. President Obama was quoted as saying, "I pretty much do that face at least once a day."

All it took was one meme to capture our collective cultural sentiment. I believe it also captures well our current moment of evangelical Christian faith in our country. For many us, the church no longer impresses. We know many reasons people are turned off to the church. We have witnessed the evangelical church's cultural, theological, and political misalignments. White evangelicalism in America in particular has caused many to take pause and grieve at how Christianity has indeed been reduced to a meme.

With pastors and church leadership being a sort of "first" disciples in the leading of churches, how do we ourselves not grow cynical or weary? What do we do with the increasing numbness and lack of being impressed?

We have a presumptuous role in the world of faith and religion, commissioned to point the world to heavenly signs and moments for people to see and believe and put their trust in the Lord. Will we be able to see the signs that Jesus brings when they are before us? We will need our eyes continually trained and attuned by God's Spirit through the Scriptures. Just as there are a multiplicity of signs in the Scriptures pointing us toward Christ's story, God gives us multiple signs of how this story unfolds in our world today.

Our hearts and eyes need to be trained to go further into the mystery, miracle, and wonder. We require an interpretive lens, an inquisitive heart that asks, What about God and the nature of Christ's kingdom are being revealed to us here in this moment? We can begin the conversation by (1) interpreting heavenly data in real time through questions about dance and dirge and (2) seeing how the Table of Christ gives us fertile ground for engaging suffering in redemptive ways.

LOOK, THERE GOES CHRIST!
INTERPRETING THE HEAVENLY DATA

Jesus knew that signs and miracles would not create instant believers. Miracles are miracles because, well, they are not commonplace. But witnesses to these miracles could be either receptive, indifferent, or indignant. Jesus' performance as Messiah even had a way of grating on the religious establishment of the day. On more than one occasion Jesus even found himself confronting demands for explanations of the miracles or simply challenging the doubting soul. One fateful day, Jesus' cousin John would be no exception.

John was a man of deep faith, a career prophet, a forerunner and apocalyptic preacher, with his life's work pointing back to Christ and the coming judgment. But on this day his vocation came into momentary question. He had lingering memories of the Jordan River, where he saw the Messiah in a deeper revelation while he declared, "Look, the Lamb of God, who takes away the sin of the world!" (John 1:29). Now his current station in life was not as triumphalist as he had perhaps hoped.

In prison, John found himself looking for clarity—a confirmation about Jesus' actions in keeping with messianic credentials. While the text doesn't exactly describe John's mental state, John's question was telling, as was Jesus' non-sentimental response. Jesus provided a window into the nature of the kingdom of Christ, showing how the work of the Messiah was to be located as an extension of how heaven meets earth.

> Go back and report to John what you hear and *see*: The blind receive sight, the lame walk, those who have leprosy are cleansed, the deaf hear, the dead are raised, and the good news is proclaimed to the poor. Blessed is anyone who does not stumble on account of me. (Matthew 11:4-6)

Jesus was speaking about deep transformations at the breakdowns—the places where Christ's wonders are the most obvious.

"I am here, the kingdom is here, and here's how it works here on earth as it is in heaven."

Jesus' words pointed to Jubilee, a form of cosmic reset. And this announcement would not include the fanfare that many Jews rightfully expected. There was no triumphalist entry, at least in the way they expected. No grand inauguration. The acts of Jesus operated in ways traditional empire and kingdom did not.

WITNESSING HEAVENLY INVITATIONS: THE DANCE AND THE DIRGE

After his discourse about John the Baptist's special calling and intersection in redemptive history, Jesus spoke about people's unresponsiveness to heaven in their midst:

Whoever has ears, let them hear.

To what can I compare this generation? They are like children sitting in the marketplaces and calling out to others:

"We played the pipe for you,
  and you did not dance;
we sang a dirge,
  and you did not mourn."

For John came neither eating nor drinking, and they say, "He has a demon." The Son of Man came eating and drinking, and they say, "Here is a glutton and a drunkard, a friend of tax collectors and sinners." But wisdom is proved right by her deeds. (Matthew 11:15-19)

Jesus compares his current skeptical, doubting generation to children in a marketplace. We can almost get an image of children running around a mall, excitedly and distractedly, with much drawing their attention. This remark about children was in deep contrast to Jesus' other claim about children in Matthew 19:14, where he says, "Let the little children come to me, and do not hinder them, for the kingdom of heaven belongs to such as these."

Those raising or educating children know how important framing and interpreting the moments and signs of life can be. Otherwise moments might get passed over, fleeting into an unrecorded yesterday.

At a recent Thanksgiving dinner, we were at the table with our nieces and nephews, the children doing what children do—rushing through the meal to get to the games. As futile as our efforts might have seemed in finally wrangling their attention, my wife and I took time to remind them of the moment's significance.

"Look, we don't get to see family often, so we cherish these beautiful moments. They remind us of God's goodness before us."

We reminded them of their aging grandparents and how it was important to cherish those moments. We were surprised at the children's deep attentiveness in response. We even waited for some good, curious questions to draw forth our deeper insights. At least that's what we hoped, only to hear, "So when's dessert?"

They all just pranced away in unison.

In comparing that generation to children, Jesus shows how that generation rejected both John and Jesus because they didn't satisfy their childish whims. When they wanted a dance, God gave them a dirge in John. When they wanted a dirge, God gave them a dance in Jesus. John and Jesus serve as paradigms for two elemental invitations into heavenly encounter: dance and dirge. Both paradigms necessitate responses, and both can connect people in deeper ways to heaven.

The dirge is an invitation to mourn and a way to deal with suffering and loss in all of its different forms. Followers of Christ get to know Christ in suffering while being in fellowship with him and others. Heaven on earth is where this thin space is held together seamlessly without contradiction.

Jesus teaches about the promise of heaven coming nearer to the exile when he states, "Blessed are those who mourn, for they will be comforted" (Matthew 5:4). In some way, this promise turns tragedy on its head, keeping us from the triumphalist forms of seeing God in the midst of suffering. While we hope that God will do miracles in this world and free the world from suffering, we know our faith requires entry into the furnaces of suffering—only to realize Jesus is present with us there as well.

The dance is our participation in and celebration of the sign. We get to know Christ in the glow of resurrection, in the abundance of life. Like Mary and her cousin Elizabeth, who hosted heaven in celebration, both pregnant with prophecy, receiving the signs with joy and glee.

We see heaven show up repeatedly, demonstrating how hope arrives in the midst of despair, in the midst of empire, where people are exiled with limited power or possibility. Paul once wrote in Philippians about how we can actually get to know God in both suffering and resurrection if we receive these moments and allow ourselves to be taught by them.

In our day, churches we will be challenged in how we treat the moments of life together. We might rush through the signs that are around us to get in another worship set. Yet we might find that expediency and discernment do not go together. Even we pastors can drive past the signs of God's wonder because we have been trained in the school of American entertainment, with all of us tempted into the lull of spectatorship. This is opposed to slowing down and seeing that God was here, is here, and that the ground on which we stand is sacred.

Connecting to heaven will require a wisdom from above—one that would have us holding space together as a church community. We help one another to discern heaven in our midst. The Lord's Table is one place where this can consistently happen.

TRAINING OUR EYES: CELEBRATING
HEAVENLY SNAPSHOTS AT THE TABLE

The table is one way heavenly moments are celebrated in churches. We more easily recognize Christ in his body broken through material elements like bread and wine. We can also witness God's image bearers around the table as sacraments in body, outward and visible signs of God's grace. To reduce the table to a ceremony of individual wafers and juice, a private moment between God and individuals, would be to miss the point altogether. Communion is a performance that carries with it a message for the world itself. It is one way we get to celebrate heaven right here, and heaven to come.

For our church, like countless others before us, Communion locates us in space and time in an embodied story of hope in Harlem. Consistently it will mean interpreting the table as both a mystical and a corporeal moment. Here the crucified and resurrected body of Christ, the proximity of our bodies to one another, the words of institution intersect with our current social experience.

Some years ago Chantilly Mers, our worship arts leader, preached on Communion. She helped us to consider and reimagine the biblical and social nature of Communion, sharing these words from Tom Driver:

> A sacrament cannot be "rightly administered" unless it signifies a social as well as a spiritual liberation. A sacrament must signify not merely the *idea* of liberation but its *actuality* as a work in which God and the people move against all forces of enslavement.

Administering the sacraments reintegrates in the manner in which Driver describes and extracts the social and public dimension inherently present in this holy rite, a counternarrative to an over-individualized view of the sacraments and how they are often received. Many in our church circles, whether Protestant or Catholic, have been formed by a sense of personal shame and unworthiness when approaching the table. A misinterpretation of Paul in 1 Corinthians 11 leads to an individualized interpretation of personal holiness at the table. The true richness of Paul's words, which were really about addressing social divisions within the church, are lost to some. The true story of unholiness is when the poor were left out of the table of fellowship.

At our church, as with many others I know, Communion is a deep moment of integration in the midst of the world's social fragmentation. We see Christ and one another through the breaking of bread and drinking of the cup. On Sundays, in the words of institution, we're reminded about the cost of Christ's body broken. The elements at the table hold grief, grace, and future glory—all in one moment. The table also holds many stories under the covering of Christ's life, death, and resurrection.

Communion, if "rightly administered," can be a heavenly snapshot of the way the walls of hostility are dismantled. Social divisions are brought down through a moment of mutual joining, with Christ's body as the joining place. Heavenly moments are shared at the table, as we are present in our bodies as we share in the body of Christ.

At the table we can also find intimacy and union as a church, as a sign and a challenge to break out of the anonymity of life in the big city. We have invited people into a fellowship to process their suffering in light of Christ's, since the table speaks to the whole story of Christ in the fellowship of suffering and the power of resurrection.

We also find the table can be a sign of a generous space for those who are on the journey with Christ, even those who are spiritually seeking. Through the words of institution, we remind those who haven't made a decision to follow Christ but are seeking that we join them in pondering the signs. We don't presume all people who come to church are followers of Christ. We're simply honored that they would choose our church as a space for searching. We draw quite a few unchurched people to our community. Yet we recognize the sanctity of Communion is for those who make a profession to follow Christ; therefore we encourage people to enter with full participation in that manner.

Doing Communion in a circle becomes a formative moment of diverse fellowship, working in deep contrast to, say, a NYC subway car. Strap hangers in NYC know the diversity of a subway car. Yet we also know that close proximity with people doesn't equate to fellowship. Our attempt is to help recognize how we can hold space and make room for those who haven't made a commitment to Christ. This creates a different dynamic at the table with those who are not believers. It is not an invitation to participate in the elements, but to be present with us in the circle of Communion, as an indicator that both God and the church are walking with them in their search for signs.

We find that the table, bread, and companionship help people to see Jesus more clearly. People are also encouraged to empathic sight as they look at one another breaking the bread and passing it forth. The table facilitates a form of greeting, an "I see you" moment, an acknowledgment that we are in this together. And being seen is one of the ultimate acts of presence and hospitality we can offer someone. It's an invitation to encounter heaven in its truest form; as Paul states, "For the kingdom of God is not a matter of eating and drinking, but of righteousness, peace [shalom] and joy in the Holy Spirit" (Romans 14:17).

When invisibility is conquered, the power of seeing someone in the light of Christ is divine. As a response to being seen, people might respond with a gaze. This is reminiscent of the South African response *Sibona*, which means "I am here" and "When you see me you bring me into existence." What was once invisible has materialized and has been remembered by being enfolded through God's presence in God's people. When we receive the host from one another, in gratitude, God reminds us through our togetherness that we are seen, and we have seen the signs of God.

It's amazing what the Spirit-filled gaze can do—a true moment of celebration. Our table moments are a continual invitation of celebration within God's grander story—expansive enough to also hold grief and suffering.

EYES TRAINED THROUGH SUFFERING:
AN OUTWARD-FACING TABLE

We don't commune exclusively around suffering and death, or even moments of life and joy, but we are given opportunities to intimately abide in all of these moments together. The Christian story, mediated by the sacrament, can offer us some recourse through the different seasons of life. Curating the table gives us fresh language for formative moments in the life of the church.

Sacraments can be dynamic this way. They help guide us through the seasons and transitions of life—where life in community fosters a form of intimacy. If we abide in Christ and remain in fellowship with him and one another, suffering can take on a different character. When suffering and struggle come, it can be another way to develop shared intimacy through burden sharing. When disciples extend their hands to one another through grief together it fulfills the comfort of God.

In 2012, the table of suffering was where our whole church was forged together. We were transformed by participating in my family's suffering when my wife was diagnosed with stage four lymphoma. We had received the devastating news from her oncologist on February 2. Mayra's world and our world as a family would be turned upside down in an instant. Within one day she was hospitalized for treatment. Not one day later, Mayra would have brain surgery to have a port surgically inserted into her skull where the chemotherapy could be administered.

In the midst of this we were discerning how to share and even invite people into this moment. We knew inviting people into this moment also meant inviting people into our vulnerability. People would witness us in a very raw emotional state. Yet it would be a particular fellowship created—to support our family during uncertain times. So what better place to make this invitation than at the Communion table?

The Sunday after the diagnosis, I tearfully shared our moment with the church. I used God's table as an invitation into participation in our season of suffering. Our table was extended outward with Christ's call to remember his broken body—his wounds—giving us hope that healing could come to

Mayra. The church tearfully joined me, providing us with prayers and presence.

In our wilderness journey we were tethered to a miraculous web of support from the church family. So palpable was it, in fact, that when someone asked us, "Where is God at a time like this?" God's presence never came into question. The embodied love and hope of Christ was all around us. We didn't get bogged down with existential questions. The church's presence was God's deep grace stemming from a simple yet profound question: "How can we walk, suffer, and grieve with you in this moment of unforeseen turmoil?"

The church served in every way from providing childcare to restocking our kitchen to cleaning. Our worship team brought the gift of the Spirit, presence, and warmth through music to the hospital. Music resounded with inspiration and comfort filling the Mount Sinai cancer ward. We celebrated together through suffering because we didn't grieve as those who had no hope. Celebration became a form of resistance to a narrative of an aloof God. Through each tearful strum of the guitar, through each vibrating vocal cord, we believed God was also singing with us.

Mayra's struggle was the most honest struggle I'd ever witnessed. She would be selective about the forms of encouragement that people would bring. Each visitor brought gifts with them. Our friend Richard brought large post-it notes so people could write laments and encouragements on the hospital wall. Other clergy friends brought silence, comfort, and grounded truth. Our family members brought us respite by the simple things like watching television together, cooking, or spending time in the hospital.

For eight months we would watch helplessly as Mayra endured cycle after cycle of aggressive chemotherapy treatments. Her once healthy body steadily weakened from the grueling effects of the therapy—a cocktail of poisons imposing a succession of harm with the hopes of healing her.

Yet after almost one year, thankfully, Mayra pulled through and is now in remission.

Mayra's strength, honesty, and presence to her own pain made it so that others were challenged to be present and attend to it differently. One doesn't seek suffering out—knowing that God can transform us through it was a grace Mayra embraced amid uncertainty.

Not one moment was ever lost as Mayra became an honest curator of her story of illness. Her journey to the depths gave a perspective unmatched; a visit by death's shadow provides a perspective few will ever have. Somehow two things happened: the thought of death lost its finite sting, and yet every simple moment of life became that much more precious and abundant.

The journey of illness shaped me as well. My pain opened my eyes in a particular way. In just the second week after the diagnosis, I was leaving my apartment to head to the hospital when I noticed a neighbor of mine pacing the hallway getting some exercise. I had taken slight notice of her before. But my gaze was drawn differently now.

Her gait was different. She was wearing a baseball cap to cover the loss of hair. The imagery of the cancer ward was so embedded that I noticed something different about her this time. So I stopped. I inquired whether she was okay. She shared about how she was enduring her sixth cycle of chemotherapy after being diagnosed with breast cancer. She shared how she was recovering well and remained hopeful.

I shared the news about my wife's cancer and the recent traumatic events that had happened. She began to encourage me, confirming that our choice of hospital was good, encouraging me to continue to remain positive and hopeful.

My neighbor was a sign that I had overlooked before because my eyes were not attuned or trained. Trauma had retrained my sight, making me keen to what I had missed on the same floor of my apartment building. My new sight found its way into the streets as well. I began to notice suffering of this same sort as people walked by tending to their daily lives. Bodies that had been rendered immobilized became signs that our bodies have limits, but that Christ suffered in body and that there's a hope for healing in the now and in the fullness of the kingdom to come.

Bodies can be great sources of struggle, but they can also be visible signs of how God came in body and suffered in body. In Christ "we do not have a high priest who is unable to sympathize with our weaknesses" (Hebrews 4:15). This is the same Christ of whom the Scriptures say, "By his wounds you have been healed" (1 Peter 2:24).

With heaven having its way by breaking into our world unannounced, it intersects the breaches between God's shalom and the world in need of repair. The church, if it's tuned in, gets to discern these encounters, curate them, and actively participate.

Indeed we live in a world that misses heaven and its many signs. Yet God can meet us in our suffering as a way of awakening us to heaven in different ways. We not only have a Christ who brings us heaven, but we have a Christ who walked through hell for us. Therefore suffering can have a different character in the here and now, as we look forward with hopeful imaginations.

REFLECTION QUESTIONS

1. What are the signs of life in your church community? Neighborhood? City?

2. How does your church make room for moments of celebration?

3. How can your church better curate moments of suffering?

4. What is your church's biblical view of Communion?

5. What conversations about suffering (both global and local) can be had? What are ways you can integrate the world's social reality at the Lord's Table of grace?

10

EL CULTO
MARKING LIFE'S MOMENTS, RESCRIPTING TRAUMA

El culto es el reflejo mas claro de la
teologia de la comunidad de fe.
[The church service is the clearest reflection
of a faith community's theology.]

ORLANDO COSTAS, *EL PROTESTANTISMO*
EN AMERICA LATINA HOY

The church is called, as it exists in this space of
trauma, to engage in the crucial task of reordering
the collective imagination of its people, and
to be wise and passionate in this task.

SERENE JONES, *TRAUMA AND GRACE*

CHICO HAD *MAD SKILLS* with a spray can. Crowds of us
would gather to witness colorful, vibrant mist flowing

from his spray can nozzle. Bland bricks and storefront gates were transmuted into neighborhood narratives describing the current times we were living in.

Chico attended my local Pentecostal church when I was a tween. He was an avid part of the youth group, while also maintaining his graffiti career. Chico's graffiti and murals have graced many walls in the Lower East Side of Manhattan. Not only was Chico's graffiti legendary in our neighborhood, but his talents had international reach as well.

For some people, graffiti is considered just another form of vandalism. But for many of us, graffiti served as our hood hieroglyphic, telling the world, "look and see" because we're here. Elements of hip-hop were all around us as a form of resistance to invisibility. If a person was murdered around the way, a mural would tell the story along with flowers and pictures of the deceased leaning against tall white *velas* (candles). Graffiti murals were the voice of exile, often telling a story of neglect in the heart of a lived Babylon experience—our hood artists and historians bidding us to hear the collective pulse of the disinherited.

Not long after September 11, when two planes struck the World Trade Center, Chico painted a mural with George Bush, Saddam Hussein, and Pope John Paul II standing side by side. This colorful and bright mural also had doves painted in the background with the inscription, "Make peace not memorials." A gaping hole where World Trade Centers 1 and 2 once stood tall represented the city's grief and loss. Chico's mural asseverated the collective trauma connected to 9/11, when death was fresh, while we were all reaching for our collective breath. In the meantime, Chico from the hood transcended a hood narrative into a global monument. Our city and neighborhood will remember that 2,606 souls no longer graced our planet. Chico's work served as a work of the people, preserving a living story.

A 2003 article from *Vibe Magazine* featuring one of Chico's murals stated, "When urban artists want an outlet for their views, they don't call CNN. They take it to the streets." Street artists become curators of the particular life of the hood, while also telling a more universal story of pain and the need for hope and healing.

When school budget cuts eliminate art and music programs, or when there is no creative outlet for real-time expression, street artists name reality, leaving behind a body of work. For those of us who are in gentrifying neighborhoods, becoming in touch with the stories these murals tell will give a sense of community history and pain. Graffiti can be a form of public liturgy this way, allowing communities to process life and make meaning. It's a way of marking the moments lest we rush them by.

What if church liturgy were somehow connected to our social reality this way? Liturgy shapes the work of the people, expressing the work of God in the moments of life as they happen. We get to tell stories about the mundane or monumental moments of every day, in ways that honor these moments, giving us a glimpse of God's work in our midst.

Paul once shared an intimate message with the church this way: "You yourselves are our letter, written on our hearts, known and read by everyone" (2 Corinthians 3:2). The church marks its own moments, sprays into existence its own mural through its Sunday gathering, leaving letters and stories on the walls of people's hearts.

Sundays can become spaces and places of resistance, of cultivating a resistance to glossing over trauma or even formative life moments without honoring them. Hence I'd like to offer two lenses for the church in the life and practice of its liturgy: (1) marking the moments during formative life transitions and (2) healing for an imagination out of time.

LET'S HAVE CHURCH AGAIN: MEETING AND MARKING MOMENTS WITH GOD TOGETHER

Our moments in life can either be fleeting or point to the reality of the divine in the world. Church space therefore can be used to help people mark the "on-the-way" nature of life. We can foster a rhythm where identities are affirmed and can become conformed to the life and image of Christ—with the church doing what it does best: having church.

There's no community with more opportunity than the church to interpret and curate the changing moments of life. We go through life's beginnings, middles, and ends often unaware that a story is unfolding. And a life that is fleeting has meaning only when enfolded within God's greater purposes for our lives. Doing church can actually serve an inspired role in providing compass points to help us stop, reflect on, and anchor people in God's work in the world. People can then find themselves in the story of God's work at any given moment in time.

I count myself among the many who have unfortunately downplayed the role of the Sunday gathering. I've heard all the critiques: "We should be the church and not have church." "We need to get out of the four walls." Heck, I've even invented some of my own. What can one hour and a half (three hours if you're Pentecostal) possibly be in the life of a community?

But I realize that Sundays are an opportunity to paint murals together on the walls of our collective hearts.

We invite new commitments and allegiances to Christ.

We provide spaces for reaffirmation of our calling to follow him.

We accept new members.

We baptize people into the body of Christ, the church.

We help to affirm the covenant of singleness.

We walk people through marriage vows.

We grieve together when those vows need to be upended.

We dedicate babies.

We sprinkle babies through baptisms.

We honor those called to join the church.

We honor those who have served our church and are called out to another.

We set up. We tear down. We serve fair trade . . . or *Bustelo*.

We grieve pain, even sharing in one another's burdens.

Our formation is highly dependent on how we honor the fleeting moments of life. Transitions are a way of seeing God's work in our reality. Our holy task with others, as Dr. Erica Brown writes, is to "sanctify the time, not merely pass it." God's invitation into the holy rhythms of time and life in the church allows our collective life together to be imbued with divinity from week to week.

We can facilitate how people are to encounter and interpret moments in life in light of Scripture. From past and future moments to moments happening in real time, we discover the sacred, with an invitation to cast off our shoes while standing on holy ground. We name and identify the sacred because much of our life is lived "on the way." Much of the substance of our lives happens while we are in transit.

My son had an interesting insight on the nature of fleeting moments. As we walked through Marcus Garvey Park in East Harlem we saw an art installation. On the lawn were three *imba yokubikiras*, kitchen houses, resembling ones seen in rural Zimbabwe. The installation was an obvious workmanship, transporting us to a reality thousands of miles away from our local park.

I noticed Javier pause a few yards away from the installation as he pondered it. He then asked, "Dad, isn't that just a big waste of time?"

"What do you mean?"

"The workers [artists] doing all this work just to take it down later."

[Brain buffers]

"You're right, Javier. But think about this—why do people bother decorating birthday cakes only to be gobbled by children later? Why don't people just serve a big glob of cake batter, egg and flour? Or just serve a cake without frosting or decoration? Art is there to say something special no matter how long it lives."

Even a decorated birthday cake is an icon for a moment, pointing back to a greater creative capacity, and even a creator. Our parties then become moments to mark someone's arrival into existence.

Curating these conversations is a way of interpreting moments. This is one of the distinctive gifts our leaders and preachers attempt to give our church. By way of every worship rehearsal, set up and tear down, and fleeting sermon we display tiny fragments of God's grander love. With every bulletin handed graciously, with every grace-filled gaze, truly seeing the people who enter our doors, our simple encounter marks moments on the divine chalkboard.

The *culto*, Spanish for church service, is the taproot of my imaginational vitality for the church. It's a place we corporately create opportunities, witnessing signs and wonders of the kingdom, huddling then breaking after a benediction, bringing a new reality to bear on the world. If our church *liturgia* (liturgy) and our rituals are connected to the pulse of the world, it can even help people learn "God talk," which can shape godly thinking within the encounters of everyday life.

High or low church liturgy and ritual can be formative and meaning making. If this is true, Sundays as a ritual space ought to be infused with vitality, urgency, and necessity. There's a mutuality in ritual as we interact with the divine. Ritual space, according to Nathan Mitchell, "is not only a way Christians negotiate their access to the sacred; it is also their way of editing experience, 'rewriting' personal history, and appropriating a new identity."

A good church service can string together fragmented, meaningless pieces of life in the world, crafting them into coherence by way of entering God's larger narrative. This is the power of liturgy at work. What we create and reflect on in church can permeate its way out in the world. It also shapes a new identity as God's children joined together are formed over time, rhythm, and space.

This is what we churches do fifty-two Sundays per year: we disciple others into honoring; we give moments their due gravity. Prayers are a way of transforming time this way. I recall once when one of our vocalists prayed, "God, we would be simply singing songs and entertaining people if not for you. This gathering would have no meaning if you were not here."

Our worship leaders play a prominent role in marking moments if they select songs that engage the moments and seasons of life thoughtfully. Worship can have a transcendent quality that reframes moments and allows people to find an alternative vision, even through grim circumstances. Worship can offer hope, especially when it is offering a real hope connected to, not detached from, the often-harsh realities of life.

In a volunteer-driven space where people are cycling in and out, we might wonder if it is wasteful to invest in people who say, "I'm in the church for a short season." What I've found in this reflection is that if we're open enough, every person has the potential to bring a gift to our own formation as well. It is this reciprocal blessing, and naming and honoring of moments that live through each person crossing our path, that can add blessing to the church's living mural.

HOW ARE WE WELCOMING PEOPLE IN?

As we develop paths of integration, inserting people into the life of the church body as an invitation into membership and God's particular story, let's consider how people come in.

Like many of my colleagues I make it a custom to open my home to people who have recently visited the church. I often note that this form of hospitality would never be possible if not for the Sunday service. In my living room I've hosted moments with seekers, nominal Catholics, the less religious, and those looking for a faith that communicates to their current intersection in life. We also receive transfers from other churches, where I can often be grateful for the efforts other pastors have invested in their lives.

Having new people allows us to see whether what we purport to be as a church reflects what newcomers see. Has our DNA, our organizational culture, endured the length of time? When I host guests at home some might say the experience of community matches up with what we present on our church website. These moments can serve as an affirmation. In contrast, these conversations can also help us realize that we might need mission realignment.

These lunches can mark a healthy beginning for those who are looking to become part of the family. Someone who recently came to our pastor's connection lunches and identifies as spiritual but not religious said "passing the peace" was his favorite part of the service. He was probably an extrovert.

Passing the peace is more than a mere gesture; it is a biblical and historical greeting. Passing the peace reminds people they are seen. In being beheld by someone else we are all humanized in a city where it's easy to remain anonymous. In the words of the Jewish philosopher Martin Buber, people go from being an "it" to a "thou." And no matter how shy or introverted we might be, deep down we all know moments when anonymity is overrated.

ELEGANT ENTRANCES AND BLESSED EXITS

Churches can also encourage and curate elegant entrances and blessed exits. How we enter and exit churches is vital to spiritual formation, and the church can take a page from Latino/a culture. Latino/a culture knows the mutual honoring of relationships across generations. Whenever my family visited my aunt at her home, we would ask for *la bendicion,* the blessing, upon entering and exiting. While often just a formality, it was a way to mark the moment and acknowledge that we had received something from our time together. The blessing of our elders was also the acknowledgment that God was present in our coming in and going out.

The Deuteronomic blessing "You will be blessed when you come in and blessed when you go out" demonstrates how God is involved in the daily movements of God's people (Deuteronomy 28:6). The words of the psalmist come to life when we contemplate, "Surely your goodness and love will follow [us] all the days of [our] life," at every juncture in life (Psalm 23:6). Even during a simple visit to Auntie's house.

When people are released from the church into a new season, all it takes is a pastor naming a handful of beautiful contributions made during their time at the church. It implies that the pastor was present to God's work in this person's life and was paying attention—either by direct observation or through the mindful watch of another church leader.

Why do this? Getting on God's agenda for someone is to remind them of the church's personal witness to God's goodness over their *specific* life. This is another form of pastoral authority— another way to curate with specificity God's work in God's household. We encourage the growth that we've witnessed lest no one name it. We also encourage, in faith, the new contributions to be made as people embark toward new spaces.

A good goodbye will underscore actual sacrifice and commitment. We can't overlook moments when sacred bodies once occupied sacred space in our lives and our pews. People who sat through sermons, some of them not good; participated at the Lord's Table; inspired new ideas; supported a budget; or invited other people who have remained thereafter.

Exits are difficult. And emotional immaturity can surface in the most passive aggressive of ways. I've been on both sides of this exchange, where pastors embrace people for a season, but don't know how to release their family of faith, often leading to smothering. Letting go, ironically, means having a healthy theology of embrace. Leaders need to lead by learning how to anticipate changes and losses in the life of the community. Taking people through a healthy grieving process is key. Especially if it is a small church community where people notice others.

A church culture that marks the moments of life will allow for this kind of celebration. Our church families will learn how to do exits well. And it can be a chance to normalize the passing of the seasons by marking them.

PRACTICE: HAVING CHURCH, BUILDING RESILIENCE, ORDERING OUR TRAUMATIZED MINDS

The church can not only facilitate and mark the seasons of life, but also invite people to engage trauma in healing ways. The church can help return people to a sense of time out of the repetitive thinking loops caused by trauma. Serene Jones, in her book *Trauma and Grace*, describes how people exposed to disaster can develop a "compulsion to repeat the violence." This happens when "the mind's meaning-making structures have collapsed, so it simply repeats and recycles." The brain will normally time-stamp events as they happen in life, marking each of them in a category of memory while assigning it meaning. But in a traumatic event, the information is too fast and too furious to process, and so it "wanders and consistently replays itself."

Trauma has many of us living outside of time with painful events repeating in our minds. Our pain can be ever present while we yearn for spaces grasping for the healing grace of Christ. Acknowledging our pain will then take a measure of faith and courage. Sharing it openly will also take a great measure of trust. The church can prayerfully be a place where this happens as another pathway to healing justice, mending the broken places.

Being privy to collective traumas in life places the church in a very intimate proximity to others, in ways other institutions will not be. From traumas like disease, sudden death, domestic violence, or even divorce, church communities are often invited into the sacred task of caring for the wounded body and soul. Our church services will be most healing when they engage both personal and social ruptures, providing a sense of perspective and meaning through God's story.

One of the most rupturing and traumatizing weeks for many in and outside of the church came the week of July 4, 2016, when a young black man named Philando Castile was shot and killed by police in Minnesota while his fiancée, Diamond Reynolds, recorded the event from the passenger side in horrid disbelief. To make matters worse there was a four-year-old in the back seat.

Not one day later, Alton Sterling, another black man, was shot and killed in Louisiana from an encounter with police over selling CDs. He was wrestled to the ground and shot six times. Not long afterward we could all feel the pain through our social network newsfeeds and timelines. Many of us were in utter disbelief, not even reaching the point of lament. Replaying the videos of the shootings acted to simultaneously shock us and further numb us to such an incalculable reality.

To compound the tragedy, during a rally against police brutality, five police officers were killed by a gunman, leaving our country and our churches to ponder a string of events that many could not hope to process.

How do we walk the simultaneous grief between communities of color and those who have family members in law enforcement that police them? Pastors all over the country found themselves inhabiting these liminal spaces, knowing that people connected to all parts of these stories attended their churches.

Just days after the tragedies I received a phone call from Tanya, who attends our church. Her husband is a sergeant in the Yonkers police force, and she was afraid for his life. She invited the church to pray and stand with her family. Trauma, after all, is not selective in its impact. We can confront the reality of the misuse of power in the policing of black and brown communities while prayerfully supporting and guiding those who work in law enforcement.

Tanya described how social networks had only compounded her fear for her husband's safety. Click-of-the-button newsfeeds were triggers for replaying the trauma. Our brains are not capable of holding the senselessness of the world's pain, or processing compounded pain and atrocity in such frequent measure. For people of color in particular, looking to the traditions of courageous churches that can help us brave and withstand the difficult moments becomes an act of self-care.

The church serves best when it creates an alternative sound bite to the misguided or one-dimensional media narratives. We can participate in grief together, praying for God to intervene in the midst of our own limitations. I find that liturgies and prayers inspired by people responding to the here and now, the overwhelming present, can be powerful instruments for processing harrowing situations.

Michael K. Washington, associate pastor at New Community Covenant Church, was able to share a resource with other pastors. We adapted this litany for our context to include the family of police officers too. Here's an excerpt of the litany:

Oh, God, hear and answer us.

Today we pray for the fallen, that their names would be remembered as you recall them, that their stories would be among your best-told ones, and that their deaths might inspire us to fix broken law enforcement programs, to turn from the error of all hatred seen and unseen. In our pain we ask for your enduring mercy.

Oh, God, hear and answer us.

This morning we pray for those who have fallen from bullets by police this last week: for Alton Sterling and Philando Castile and other victims of excessive force, such as the five Latinos overlooked but also killed by police this week: Vinson Ramos, Melissa Ventura, Anthony Nuñez, Pedro Villanueva, and Raul Saavedra-Vargas. For every family involved, that your grace would be as overwhelming as their grief, that your kindness would envelop each one like a protest, and that your tears would mingle with ours as we suffer. In our pain we ask for your enduring mercy.

Oh, God, hear and answer us.

Today we pray for those Dallas police officers who were murdered this week: Lorne Ahrens, Michael Krol, Michael Smith, Brent Thompson, and Patrick Zamarripa. For Dallas Police Chief David O. Brown, who is African American and a fourth-generation Dallas native, dedicated to reducing the use of force by officers in encounters with citizens.

Oh, God, hear and answer us.

Today we pray for the perpetrators of violence, be they police, children, racists, politicians, citizens, people we love, or people we hate. Will you do the impossible and the unthinkable and save them in every just way? In our pain we ask for your enduring mercy.

When liturgy is connected to social reality it situates the church to become a more accurate interpretive timepiece in the moment. For we act not out of naiveté or numbing disconnection, but from a hope that God is with us in the muck and the mire of our times. We all need to be reminded that God works from within places of suffering, not at a safe distance.

How pastors and churches step into church spaces can bring moments of healing into a community. These moments are necessary when injury has happened to a particular community. We can stand in unity and grace together as I have witnessed churches do.

During this challenging time, some churches from the East Coast Conference of our denomination, the Evangelical Covenant Church, responded as a community of support and hope. We gathered together to grieve, pray, and sing together, and to read the names of the many, many who had lost their lives at the hands of law enforcement.

After poignant prayers, words of hope, and singing, I was about to exit the gathering when a powerful healing moment took place. Peter Ahn, a Korean American pastor, read from Ephesians, the portion about the church being one body with many parts. Peter leads a majority–Korean American yet increasingly diverse church in Englewood, New Jersey. Peter's testimony and prayer that day was really an extension of his own journey dating back to a decision from when he first planted Metro Community Church in New Jersey. Metro could've chosen to remain in Fort Lee to minister to a mostly Asian demographic. Instead the church he leads has taken deliberate efforts to join the community narrative of Englewood, where there is more of a diverse representation of black and brown folks, thereby including more of the neighborhood in the church.

As Peter prayed that day, he began with a powerful confession, catching many of us by hopeful surprise. He confessed how in his experience Koreans had often taken on a passive role in supporting black and brown lives. Many of us were in tears, perhaps unconscious about how hearing this confession proved healing for the many black and brown folks represented in the room. Peter recognized the power of the church as sacred ground for healing and racial justice, honoring a real-time moment of pain and disinheritance.

What if the church could take more risks this way? Justice and healing won't need to be mutually exclusive but go hand-in-hand. The church doesn't need to sacrifice its role in meaning making as an agent of God's truth. We hold a story too valuable, a gospel that is too good not to proclaim, a gospel that reorders our sense of time and place. This allows us to find ourselves held in the story of God's love and grace, where we have meaning and receive healing in Christ.

Our liturgies can invite God's healing presence to help people find their footing when lost. To grieve with those who grieve. To process our own grief through prayers and laments, praying for Holy Spirit resilience when we find ourselves at the end of ourselves.

What is the alternative to a church gathering that touches heaven while standing on earth? A church service that is aloof and acting out of time like one I visited shortly after. In hopes of not having to lead a service while getting a reprieve, I attended a church service in another part of town. What I found was a major production, with auditorium lights shining brightly in multiple colors. It was a surreal experience. One could get lost in the worship, which was a good feeling. The sermon was therapeutic—individually tailored toward people's personal pursuits. One could leave feeling blessed about one's own possibilities going forth into the world. But somehow the church succeeded at creating a hermetically sealed reality. They were out of time and out of tune with the pain right outside their doorstep.

Amos the prophet from Judah reminds us of how Israel's liturgy was also removed from their own social reality, to the point that God had both deplored it and dismissed it. Judah had neglected the poor while maintaining their religious festivals, so singing and musicianship had actually become an abomination. And it was not a matter of quality or musicianship, but a community acting out of God's time and priorities. Amos 5:21-24 states,

> I hate, I despise your religious festivals;
>> your assemblies are a stench to me.
> Even though you bring me burnt offerings and grain
>> offerings,
>> I will not accept them.
> Though you bring choice fellowship offerings,
>> I will have no regard for them.
> Away with the noise of your songs!
>> I will not listen to the music of your harps.
> But let justice roll on like a river,
>> righteousness like a never-failing stream!

In *The Cross and the Lynching Tree*, James Cone describes how people had church in the Jim Crow South and after the dismissal and benediction went ahead with a ritual that was contra gospel. Many would attend the lynching of black bodies on a Sunday afternoon. Somehow the church had missed the words of another prophet named Micah, who speaks about true worship when he says,

> He has shown you, O mortal, what is good.
>> And what does the LORD require of you?
> To act justly and to love mercy
>> and to walk humbly with your God. (Micah 6:8)

Our focus on church production—no matter how good we feel when we participate—can stymie God's work through the church, because life in the church has been reduced to a form of entertainment or distraction.

What does it look like when our church services are actually engaging personal and public sin? How much more important does church space become when we're naming and framing reality in light of God's good news for the world? Our church service with our liturgies can be a place where we become a companion to people through the different transitions of life. The mystical nature of this gathering is that through it God can reset people's steps, honoring the moments of life in all of its grandeur, glory, and grit.

We can host spaces where Jesus can meet us at our place of trauma with the good news of the gospel, relocating us through the limbo of trauma's timeless existence. The church at its best can help us locate our bearings in a world that would disconnect us from the here and the now.

While the church is not a therapist, we can reclaim our tools for healing, recovering the power of public prayer, confession, and well-crafted litanies. They have a way of helping us make meaning of our lives in a world that continues to hold walls of hostility along racial and political divides.

We don't bypass trauma. But the function of the church as ritual space is to bring people from "rituals of denial to rituals of remembrance." We can face the pain of the world best when remembering God's own grief in the midst of it, as well as God's goodness in the hope of resurrection. We can participate in the rebirthing of a hopeful imagination in a world where it is so easy to lose it.

We also know that Christ is present in our grief, who in his body took on the deep trauma of crucifixion. Yet Christ's resurrection shows that the worst punishment inflicted on the body of Christ could not overcome the power of God's love and presence, his identification with the afflicted. People do not have to be exiled in their pain, but can be blessed by a God who is there and present through the community of believers. May the work of the people point to this healing justice and God's resurrection power.

REFLECTION QUESTIONS

1. How would you describe your church's liturgy? Organic? Semi-structured? Extremely structured? Describe why and how.

2. What can our churches do to better engage new people who come through our doors?

3. How are we providing blessing to those who are on their way out?

4. How can we as leaders be overall more present to the different traumas happening in the life of the body of the church? How can our Sunday space hold that pain?

5. For churches (even small churches without full-time worship coordinators), what kind of plans can be made

midweek to consider how liturgy can connect to world's events, or events in your community?

6. Describe a time people from church truly encouraged and supported you. How did you see Christ in these actions?

11

APOCALYPSE
CHURCH FROM A DIFFERENT VANTAGE POINT

Love in action is a harsh and dreadful
thing compared to love in dreams.

FYODOR DOSTOYEVSKY, *THE BROTHERS KARAMAZOV*

Is it possible that we all love compassion and
justice . . . until there's a personal cost to living
compassionately, loving mercy and seeking justice?

EUGENE CHO

Sit down, be humble.

KENDRICK LAMAR

AT LEAST EVERY OTHER NIGHT I dream the world comes
to an end. Well, if not *the* world, my little world at least.
The story is always the same, unfolding in different forms—like a

provincial apocalypse—a catastrophe in my childhood neigh-borhood. In one instance the East River takes on tsunami form, covering and sweeping through my old neighborhood. The only thing left standing, of course, are the housing projects, which along with our roaches can survive nuclear holocaust.

In my more grandiose dreams I find myself in Paul Revere mode, riding to warn others of impending doom. And yes, I fully recognize that once upon a time, prior to the Broadway hit *Hamilton*, the thought of a Puerto Rican riding on horseback in co-lonial attire would have been a stretch . . . yet the times do shift.

I also know that my personal angst has quite the fellowship. Apocalypse seems to be a shared, unconscious anxiety across the larger human family. We don't have to look far—one can easily detect it through the means of cinema. Hollywood is replete with scripts and storylines about the end of the world, from blowing up NYC to rescuing it from stray comets or alien forces from far-away galaxies or dimensions, or the popular script of lone sur-vivors as the hope of humanity who fight off virus-infected zombies. Wherever these familiar storylines go, people's fears (and fascinations) have a way of rearing their heads above the unconscious. The world anticipates the reset button, and some, like Swiss psychologist Karl Jung, believe that there's something apocalyptic written into the collective unconscious.

Apocalyptic writing is somewhat different from any uncon-scious pattern hardwired into people. In the Jewish world, this form of writing brought revelation to life. "This way of writing was designed to correspond to, and make available the visions and 'revelations' seen by holy, prayerful people who were wrestling with the question of the divine purpose." God essentially lifts the veil for the Jewish exiles, showing them what was and what was to come.

During the time of John's Apocalypse, otherwise known as Revelation, Christians were experiencing hostility under Roman rule. The church was desperately seeking encouragement, seeking God's activity in the midst of it all. According to Brian Blount in *Can I Get a Witness?*, the apostle John desired for the church

> to stand out and stand apart from the expected show of deference to Roman lordship. John was essentially asking his people to pick a social and religious fight.... Above all, as the Lord's representatives, they are to initiate his victory by living out a witness of active and aggressive resistance against any power, human or supernatural, that would contest his lordship by establishing and promoting its own.

An apocalyptic reading of culture helps the church to see the social and religious "fights" it must engage. This perspective can benefit the church to be resistant to the powers of this world. We can begin to discern, identify, and name false symbols of our collective security so they are dismantled and exposed.

Christianity in America in many ways has participated in an unconscious extension of colonialism. Blurred boundaries between government and church have caused our country to often mistake the Manifest Destiny for the Great Commission. Our symbols of American pride and might have galvanized unholy unions, revealed in American flags draped over the cross of Christ on many pulpits. Other symbols and idols reveal our sacralizing of guns. We saw this clearly on December 4, 2015, in Jerry Falwell Jr.'s convocation address at Liberty University, an evangelical school, where he encouraged students to bear arms against the so-called threat of their Muslim neighbors.

Apocalypse can expose our central symbols and idols and points us back to our true help in God. Therefore apocalypse is for us, the church, as the church can place itself within the world correctly, back to holy alignment and faithfulness.

Our world's problems are not calling for new church models as much as churches situated humbly and prophetically in the world. By conforming our wills, allowing God to shape even our dreams and visions of church ministry, we will see ourselves as a church properly located as part of the common humanity of the world. We will practice a love that combats idealism and illusion, the kind of love that does ministry with people away from an idealized approach.

As we ponder an apocalyptic reading of culture—the twilight of the American evangelical church and its influence—there are symbols and patterns requiring dismantling: (1) *symbols of sentimentality through mission,* where the idea and excitement of shalom and unity is greater than the actual effort and pursuit of it, and (2) *symbols of heaven from above,* where ministry somehow is performed above, disconnected from context. This is the challenge of the church now; it was also the consistent challenge of churches in the first century.

CONFRONTING SYMBOLS OF
SENTIMENTALITY: LOVE GONE ALOOF

The book of Revelation contains admonitions and encouragements to seven different churches. The church of Ephesus was
called out for what Bible students remember most: abandoning
their first love.

What did it mean for the church to fall out of love with God?
I can already hear the debates as we listen to these questions
with our modern ears. Our church traditions and leanings will
lead us to different responses, asking, What does this love refer
to? Will it mean more fervent worship? Adding more personal
prayer time and fellowship with God? Serving the world, because after all "we have to do something"? These are all healthy
elements to integrate into our churches, of course.

Yet according to N. T. Wright, "'Love,' in the early Christian sense,
is something you *do*, giving hospitality and practical help to those
in need, particularly to other Christians who are poor, sick or
hungry. That was the chief mark of the early church, and the best
advertisement for, faith in this God." The marks of love were holy
actions aligned with God's heart and priorities. While it sounds
simple enough, simplicity can get subsumed through the idols
and distractions of the culture—which is partially the point of
these letters to the various churches. Love can be redefined and
expressed in many ways that might appear to be love, but these
miss the mark when no longer in alignment with God's heart.

Love goes astray when it becomes something less than it's supposed to be. Like churches before us we must endeavor to reclaim

what true love is today. Christianity in America can suffer its own romanticized view of love. In some ways romanticism can make hazy the way we approach the greatest commandments:

> "Love the Lord your God with all your heart and with all your soul and with all your mind." This is the first and greatest commandment. And the second is like it: "Love your neighbor as yourself." All the Law and the Prophets hang on these two commandments. (Matthew 22:37-40)

Love for one another and love for neighbor was a mark of the first church, and it would be expressed in a Spirit-led overflow of love, taking them beyond the boundaries of Jerusalem and Judaism. But love regrettably can be substituted with a false sense of piety that negates this public witness. We might wonder today what a lesser love looks like in the North American church. Some have identified it as sentimentality.

Theologian Stanley Hauerwas once wrote, "The great enemy of the church today is not atheism but sentimentality." Sentimentality can look like an over-the-top emotional attachment to love, an attachment that becomes a romantic driving force, where one can fall in love with the idea of changing the world but go no further to fulfill the demands. Sentimentality is often the notion of falling in love with love, but shirking from the efforts involved in loving well.

Sentimentality isn't always easy to identify in the church. But I find it can be seen more easily through symbolic action. For one, it's the evangelical church's tendency to romanticize justice.

Sentimentality can produce an illusion that we are truly connected to others in love, and even worse, that we are truly sharing a collective burden as the body of Christ. In our Indiegogo society we can feel that a mere click keeps us connected to the issues on the ground, or that speaking out on something in social networking will somehow garner change.

Eugene Cho, author and pastor of Seattle Quest Church, makes this notion concrete through his own confession: "I admit to being more in love with the idea of changing the world . . . than actually changing the world." It's a confession I've had to make myself time and again as someone who leans into being an idealist.

The church can be of communal and public good when it goes beyond romantic mission slogans and websites that showcase our service to the poor. When sentimental love converts into sacrifice, it can better take on the character and shape of the cross of Christ. Those who witness and are on the receiving end of such love can begin to see and believe and put their trust in the Lord, because God is present to them through God's church.

With "love in action" as opposed to a "love in dreams," churches might even find themselves on the losing end of things, like the first church often did. Persecuted. Maligned. Placed at odds with the powers of this world. In contrast, churches that neglect their first love will be those whose love for God and people is misaligned and misappropriated. Their actions will be a distortion of the greatest commandments—as happened more recently through First Baptist Dallas.

FIRST BAPTIST DALLAS AND THE WORSHIP
OF AMERICAN SENTIMENTALITY

When the church attempts to find itself on the winning side of empire we will witness unholy alignments with people in power, with a compromised love for God. Never was this more apparent than in First Baptist Dallas on July 1, 2017, at their Celebrate Freedom concert. While under the banner of celebrating our veterans, the symbols and the imagery of the event were what was disturbing. A large American flag loomed behind a choir as they sang "Make America Great Again." Very shortly after this event, the song would be copyrighted by the Christian Copyright Licensing International (CCLI). Witnessed that day was a platform propped up by the fear of the loss of religious freedom and the hope that somehow President Trump would restore these rights for the evangelical church in this country.

Jonathan Aigner, a writer for Patheos, opined,

> It seems innocent enough. Indeed, if it were just another little ditty to whistle on Independence Day, it would be fairly innocuous.... The problem is that it has been adopted by a significant portion of the evangelical church.... Pledging allegiance to God and to America in the same breath, melding together the kingdom of God and self, they pray a blasphemous prayer to a red, white and blue Jesus.... How tragically this prayer cancels out the prayer of Jesus himself. The political church prays, "Make America great

again!" Jesus prayed, "Your kingdom come. Your will be done, on earth as it is in heaven."

The church loses its prophetic witness when a form of nationalism and self-preservation dilutes love. This is a misguided posture that ensures the church remains on the winning side of things. Lamentably, it is a mistaken view of what true triumph is. For the historical church has been at its best when its alignment is shaped by a nonviolent, noncoercive, persuasive love led by Christ's Spirit in the world, ultimately untethered to government authorities.

The concert demonstrated an extreme sentimentality—American Romanticism mixed with a diluted form of Christianity. When the church makes itself at home in these spaces it gives in to the illusion that God has somehow made our country exceptional: a historically dangerous theology, and a twisted form of triumph.

Like our churches today, the church of Ephesus was called to repent and return to its first love, to return to doing the things it had done first. Thankfully, there are many outposts of resistance across the country and globe today attempting to reclaim their first love. There are stories and snapshots of kingdom courage that can inspire us to love well in our context, in ways that are not idealized or sentimental, where local efforts can meet larger issues. Pantego Bible Church is a shining example of this kind of place.

PRACTICING CHRIST'S DISRUPTIVE LOVE:
PANTEGO BIBLE CHURCH, DALLAS

Pantego Bible Church experienced how cross-shaped love will disrupt a church, and in some instances even downsize it. Jesus is familiar with this, as he once downsized a "church" crowd in his day. Just think about the miracle of the fish and the loaves in John 6. In one gaze Jesus has compassion on the crowds that followed him. Jesus would feed each and every person indiscriminately through the miracle of multiplying the fish and loaves. Yet not a few verses later, he would downsize this community that had romantic ideas of making him king by force in an effort to overthrow Rome.

Whenever the nature and the character of the kingdom were misinterpreted, Jesus would somehow disrupt and sometimes downsize. Whenever ministers of God reintroduce the nature of the kingdom of God it can cause extreme controversy, even causing the end of a church as the leader knows it. The politics of Christ will disrupt the status quo and even be dismissed as social and liberal in our day. But really, it's a full gospel that takes seriously how love is not love without social concern.

One day in 2009, Pastor David Daniels of Pantego Bible Church encountered two African refugees from Burundi at his door. Turns out they were also pastors who were inquiring if Pantego Church could allow them worship space in their outdoor area. Pastor Daniel would instead give this congregation of 150 a space indoors—in a Christlike posture and use of church space. Pastor Daniel's church was beginning to form an ecology connected to

God's heart, the place where people meet with Jesus at the margins of society.

Pantego Church would later resist the xenophobic rhetoric coming from the White House and certain parts of Congress at that time. David Montero of the *LA Times* covered the story in 2017:

> The political DNA of his church, by Daniels' measure, is GOP. With exit polls showing 81% of white evangelical Christians supporting President Trump in November, he figured most at Pantego Bible Church voted for the Republican, too. Still, he challenged his congregation to not follow the president's path. Since Daniels' arrival in 2005, about 300 attendees have left the church for a variety of reasons— a handful over displeasure with his refugee policy.

Pastor Daniel continues to share the disruptive good news of the gospel from his pulpit, stirring up the church space by extending love in the most unsentimental of ways. I believe this is the kind of disruptive love Jesus ushered in when he said, "I did not come to bring peace, but a sword" (Matthew 10:34). Jesus' vision was about upheaval—people shedding their comfortable shells of allegiance for the chafing of a daily cross. This love reorders society's cultural logic of how we approach neighbors and strangers in our world.

Further, here's how proximity to this family of refugees shaped Pastor Daniel's heart. In 2015 Daniel would adopt a family and house them. Another couple in the church would then be inspired to adopt a seventeen-year-old refugee from Tanzania, describing how "living with a refugee opened up them up to a different level of understanding."

This is what happens when the church embodies love and becomes decentered as an institution into relationship and proximity to others. Unconditional love is not a coercive work, or a romantic one. But it is a holy work that the church is called to. Love is a work that can even shape the heart of a congregation once indifferent to refugees and strangers in their midst.

Love at work will cultivate a new imagination in its gentle patience. It also opens the gates to the messiness and beauty of love and partnership. We can begin to do ministry with people through the beauty of partnership in ways that will continually surprise us. A Spirit-led enterprise for sure, the church will continually need an empowered form of guidance that would have us take on a posture of learning and doing *with* others.

MINISTRY *WITH*, NOT ABOVE:
THE SPIRIT-EMPOWERED CHURCH

Having the same attitude as that of Jesus Christ, our church ministries can be shaped by the cross in such a way as to do church *with* people instead of *to* people. This is in contrast to being performance driven or aloof, as we fight against a form of disconnection called "living above place."

Paul Sparks, Tim Soerens, and Dwight Friesen describe living above place as the "tendency to develop structures that keep cause and effect relationships far apart in space and time where we cannot have firsthand experience of them." With all of the demands of church ministry, budget meetings, board meetings, and ministry to our congregations, it is easy to default into a form of church away from the relational engagement that true love would require.

When churches repent, become decentered, finding themselves back in the "lowly" location of a servant, we can become reacquainted with the work of the Holy Spirit. Just as the first church was led to preach the gospel outside of its typical circles, we can become reacquainted with cause and effect relationships in our communities.

The Spirit's work is the ultimate symbol of partnership as our advocate and help. The Spirit's help is not just for individual empowerment, but is the collective power of the Spirit-filled church. A church in the Spirit comes alongside and advocates and helps and walks with people, decentering us to cultivate a new insight with the Spirit's facilitating presence.

Churches will act in love from a decentered place in the world, not as a flagship in our communities but as part of a fellowship. We become advocates for God's kingdom because this is the power and very definition of what Jesus left us.

Like good facilitators, the church can begin to bond (build its community within) and bridge (build capital flowing out), and become a powerful force at the breaches of our society. Bridging breakdowns in our regions will require a collaborative posture that opens us up to a new imagination beyond what we perceive to be as family.

The Spirit works not through coercion but through influence and persuasion, moving alongside and encouraging growth, wholeness, and wisdom. The Spirit is the humble partner convicting the world of sin (but not condemning) and reminding the church of Christ's posture of humility. Just as the Spirit in the eternal dance of the Trinity is continually pointing to the humility of Jesus, so is the church to follow in the footsteps of this humility.

Part of the leadership philosophy is doing ministry *with*, not *to*. There's a subtle nuance here. Doing ministry *with* implies a type of relationship, becoming a hub for bringing people together—in a sense, becoming community brokers. We can cultivate a relational capital that can leverage partnerships in the community.

For many churches around the world, the focus will no longer be on just building churches, but cultivating churches that foster ecologies. We don't just build churches; we participate in flourishing, both inside and outside of our church spaces. We participate in prayerful collaboration to seed and cultivate healthy conditions for connection.

Seeing ourselves through a different lens—that of cultivators in presence and relationship—implies that we help to foster conditions that allow for flourishing to happen. Creating conditions is an altogether different matter than seeking a final outcome. When the church as a collective exercises this form of faith, it breaks down the barriers between itself and the immediate community. The following are some short stories of churches doing ministry from this Spirit-led vantage point.

PRACTICE: FACILITATING FAITH: CHURCHES
AND THE NEIGHBORHOOD ECOLOGY

Once upon a time, church spires stood as the tallest structures in our communities, but now they have long been overshadowed by skyscrapers and Western ingenuity. We realize time and again under the shadows of so-called progress that the church will continually need to discern its own displacement and diminishment in the world—not to its own detriment but to true devotion to Christ.

No matter the size, what does a healthily decentered, diminished church look like? A church that is socially located, addressing the broken transactions at the breakdown. A church led in the ministry of the Holy Spirit, becoming a hub for healing the diseased transactions, economic turmoil, racism, and distance from God, facilitating connections with God and people in the neighborhood.

Sparks, Soerens, and Friesen have a picture of this:

> Your parish is a relational microcosm that helps bring many cause-and-effect relationships back together again. Being in collaborative relationships in real life (where you live, work, and play) awakens you to the effects of your actions both on people and on the place itself. It creates a context where your church can see whether their faith is more than just talk. The local place becomes the testing ground, revealing whether you have learned to love each other and the larger community around you.

What is described here is not classical evangelism as we have known it, but something just as rich. It's love, justice, and collaboration as an expression of evangelism in relationship to our neighborhoods. It's a new way of seeing as we are bridging relationships as an apologetic for the gospel, forming relationships that didn't exist before.

Only a decentered church has this distinctive vantage point. Most of us who have led or been a part of churches of color have been living this vantage point for years. So this isn't a *new frontier* but rather a return to the practices of the empowered oppressed.

For many pastors this will trump the question of what new programs we can begin in our context, especially here in NYC. Especially where we already have an overabundance of institutions. In this context, our role becomes more about sustaining a web of health, and not necessarily just about developing a nonprofit arm for the church.

Rather, this is how church life on a Sunday can be a part of the lifeblood of the community. I hearken back to my old Assemblies of God church, which knew how to stay, fellowship with the suffering, and connect to the grit of the time. We can consider this from several places.

Inviting. Many Latino/a Pentecostal churches invite Teen Challenge graduates to have them testify. Teen Challenge is a faith-based drug rehabilitation program. I took it for granted then, but I realize now the power of this proximity. The church removes obstacles between itself and the issues, using the Sunday space for joining and hosting neighbors. In many ways the Pentecostal church has long recognized the transformative power of the gospel at work in church space while being hospitable to the social challenges represented just down the block.

Similar invitations come through places like Resurrection Church in East Harlem, pastored by Rev. Kimberly Wright, a native Harlemite. Every month Kimberly opens the church's doors for an event called My Father's Kitchen, where the church eats together with neighborhood residents of East Harlem. This fosters a wonderful proximity to neighbors, while also utilizing the church space to break down relational barriers.

Partnering. We can take our cues from historical churches like Abyssinian Baptist Church in Harlem, engaging in proximity to the criminal justice system in participating with Fordham University's program to mentor those who have been recently released from prison. With class divides often perpetuated by the middle-class church, we will often be disconnected from people returning from prison. This program puts church members in connection with the formerly incarcerated through one-on-one mentoring. It's also a way of negotiating spaces of connection outside of a Sunday church service.

Collaborating. Rev. Michael Carrion of the Promised Land Covenant Church works in the South Bronx and has been an example of facilitating structures for collaboration around educational attainment. Promised Land Covenant Church seamlessly weaves what happens in their charter school, Promised Land Academy, with the life of the church. Michael has pastoral staff working in the charter school, therefore shaping a leadership culture that remains connected to the challenges of the educational system.

At one point in its early stages, Michael's church (like most church plants) had no youth, so they adopted a youth detention center as their youth ministry. This is a great point of consideration for younger churches starting off. Though we may quote expressions like "the poor and disavowed," people across this spectrum are sitting and worshiping together in Promised Land Covenant Church.

Seeking flourishing. Renaissance Church in Central Harlem has created a great partnership with Young Life Ministries (YLM). Asawan Morris, a director at YLM, is an associate staff pastor of Renaissance. Renaissance has created a way of integrating youth ministry in the early stages of the church's development by hosting youth at the church and through other mentoring opportunities. Now an intergenerational element is integrated into the community.

Renaissance Church has also raised money for the public school they rent as a way of showing their investment in the educational system and recognizing that the church and the school are part of a greater Central Harlem ecology.

Facilitating proximity. Exodus Transitional Community (ETC) is a faith-based nonprofit organization serving over 1,500 returning citizens per year. ETC is located in the heart of what the *New York Daily News* has called convict alley. The alley stretches south to north from 119th Street to 126th Street, west to east from Park Avenue to Third Avenue, where according to the Department of Health and Mental Hygiene the incarceration rate is more than three times the rate citywide. East Harlem represents one of the highest concentrations of people released into the community from jail and prison. And many return to prison in a cycle called recidivism.

Metro Hope Church here in East Harlem partners with ETC to facilitate proximity with other churches, educating them on matters of criminal justice and giving tours of the Exodus program as well as the so-called convict alley in East Harlem. This partnership continues to expand ETC's donor base through the church, developing generative connections and deepening partnerships with the faith community.

This initiative brings together several streams of church ministry (evangelism, justice, and discipleship). We prefer this work to remain in the hands of the church as opposed to a parachurch or nonprofit organization, which is often far from church rhythms and presence. Metro Hope Church in partnership with Exodus Transitional Community will be providing seven mentors for a group of men recently released from prison. The church will provide Metro cards for job interviews, their first tailored suit for an interview, haircuts, journals, Bibles, and other relevant things needed for successful reentry. In this group, Metro's mentors will be covering topics vital for a successful transition from prison, including resume building, budgeting, StrengthsFinder, knowing your rights, fatherhood, and faith, to name a few. The culmination of these eight to ten weeks will take place at a Sunday potluck gathering.

Incubating. Dr. Raymond Rivera began a holistic ministry center in the South Bronx named Latino Pastoral Action Center (LPAC) over twenty-five years ago. LPAC has been responsible for incubating dozens of faith-based ministries, mentoring ministers that are leaders in our city today. LPAC has assisted in the cultivation of ministries such as Youth Ministries for Peace and Justice; Angels Unaware, a nonprofit that works with young people with developmental disabilities; and Latino Leadership Circle, which provides a circle of support for bivocational ministers, as well as young, emerging Latino/a leaders in New York City.

A bivocational bridge. Redeemer Presbyterian Church Planting Center in NYC has realized the benefit of nurturing bivocational pastors in the urban context, creating a bivocational church planter pipeline called City to City. Much of the strategy is now focused on the outer boroughs of NYC, affirming pastors who might not have formal seminary education, but who seek ministry tools that could leverage the great work they're doing in their own neighborhoods. Robert Guerrero, director of City to City, together with his team, continues to strategize on how to amplify the strengths, theology, and voices of the margins.

These are signs of hope and opportunities to change for faithful and fruitful ministry and witness. Churches that recognize they are not the protagonists of their context can live out a different situatedness, bringing a humble witness in the world. Embracing apocalypse necessitates radically seeing ourselves as part of a collective humanity. Therefore Christ's commission to go out into the world will require a different vantage point for us—something that will be extremely challenging for evangelicalism as we know it.

The church decentered will mean being church from a different vantage point. Together, we can be led by the Spirit during our apocalyptic moment in history, where we love without sentimentality, taking action seriously in the world as followers of Christ. With the waning influence of our voices in our North American context, our embodied actions—welcoming strangers, holding space with diverse others, colaboring together, and forming spaces of resistance in our churches—will be a sign of the kingdom of God. Whether it means seeking healthy, vibrant churches that are doing the work, or the beginning of a new path for our churches, their downsizing, or even their closing, we know the church of God will continue to rise as long as resurrection and new life run through our DNA.

The world is seeking this radical kind of love. Will the real church please stand up?

REFLECTION QUESTIONS

1. In what ways have you detected unhealthy intersections between Christian theology, the gospel, and American thought (e.g., idealism, Manifest Destiny, individualism, capitalism)?

2. How might we have idealized or romanticized (gotten overly excited about) the work of justice in the past? What is your perspective on justice and engagement now? What shift occurred in your approach to ministry as a result?

3. If the possibility exists, what radical actions can your church take with being more hospitable to strangers with church space?

4. What conversations does your church board or leadership team need to have for fostering further proximity and collaboration with other groups in mission?

5. Let's dream together: Can you describe the potential beauty and possibility of decentering as a church in partnership with another group, ministry, nonprofit, or church? What possibilities can we see? What could we learn from those we will potentially partner with? What resources and strengths could our church contribute?

CONCLUSION

OUR CHURCH BOARD recently went through a discernment process, revisiting some core components of church identity and our continuing role in East Harlem. Our consultant posed some questions relevant to our identity, our mission, vision and values, and essentially our reach. One question she had us respond to was a complete-the-sentence exercise: "You would rather fail than become an organization that . . ."

Responding to this question was no easy matter. After some thought and prayer I wrote, "I would rather fail than become a spectator church where people simply come to 'get their fill.' I would rather fail than become a place where we lose sight of who we are, incrementally no longer taking leaps of faith."

This is how we've approached church at Metro during our ten years in East Harlem, and it is in many ways the impetus behind this book. My hope is to have provided a biblical and incarnational framework that can foster deeper conversation around Christian thought and practice for individuals and churches who would reclaim a full gospel of shalom—one that cultivates personal formation through Christ and courageous public witness, inhabiting places and contexts mindfully.

In our church and neighborhood ecologies, we can vulnerably show ourselves to others, displaying the grace that Christ has given us, a deeper integration into the world through a testimony to share as both our individual and collective vocation. When we encounter Christ, our personal narratives—our testimonies—are not subsumed by removing our scars, traumas, or even our memories. God's saving work reconstitutes our looking back so we show ourselves to others, dismantling the shame that caused us to hide, gladly pointing others in the way of Christ's restorative work.

A cross-shaped discipleship that invites us into narrow roads will be disorienting to say the least. God's invitation into the work of bridging people in the midst of difference is simultaneously sacred and disorienting, requiring a continuous posture of "here I am." What if church could factor a form of disorientation and tension into Christian formation? How could we become better guides to others?

If the church is to show up as God's experiment, a more deliberate discipleship in the form of personal and communal pilgrimage will better shape the community. This is not to be mistaken for "new frontier discipleship," which appeals to our wanderlust sensibilities to leave for new adventures, often overlooking the beauty and the broken spaces we inhabit. One question the church can engage is, How can we become God's crowdsource in our barrio? How can we live intentionally in community together as God's household, and ensure that economic gifts continue to circulate in our communities? In many places gentrification will be a consistent challenge to neighborhood narratives, as well as the displacing of the poor. How does the church see those who are the most vulnerable?

In God's plan we strive beyond the homogeneity of Babylon. We show up in the world as a diverse human community. We all hold different stories at the crossroads and intersections of community. This faith story can be traced back through Christ's life—his embodied movements—his death and resurrection. We require "new tongues," new conversational competencies that will allow us to more deeply engage one another as Christ engaged the world. We want to hear stories that can actually affect our sight, to pose better questions that will give us eyes to see how people are worlds unto themselves. This is seeing through honoring those who are before us, with empathic imaginations—Christ's vicarious love working through us.

We should also remember how we take up space in the world! Churches must be keen to how certain identities in our world unjustly hold more value than others. These realities are difficult to escape. We're mindful of how whiteness has shown up, tainting Christianity, causing malformations in how we see ourselves as people of color, immigrants, and children of the diaspora. The church must reclaim its role in honoring the image of God through minds and bodies of black, brown, and Asian image bearers, shining forth in cultural output and creativity.

When I reflect on recent shining cultural moments, I think of how the Marvel phenomenon *Black Panther* became a global movement because image bearing through Africa and the black diaspora was on global display. Witnessing my own son's glimmering eyes in the movie theater, seeing something of himself in the heroic, beautiful, intelligent, and imaginative characters on screen, did not get lost on me. To be able to see oneself in multiple variations shining in science, technology, politics, and the heroic—how is the church maintaining this sense of the sacred in deepening its vocation on matters of diversity in the church?

Inherent in this is how white sisters and brothers engage black and brown spaces. The postures of humility, divestment, and learning are paramount for healing and real reconciliation. I have too many white sisters and brothers who are engaging the journey in this reformation to doubt a revolution of hearts and values is possible.

Place is an expression of different forms of image bearing; the city for one displays the power of murals, artists leaving their mark, the laments of a community, the work of the people in the midst of disinheritance and suffering. The church can curate the voices of the voiceless as well. She can engage the question of trauma and the numerous ruptures that cause people to lose a sense of time. Churches can provide church services that curate the story of suffering differently than the world does. The tools of our trade—confession, communion, prayers, singing, and sermonizing—can be revelatory modes of true worship interlaced with social concern.

Finally, while I believe we in North America are experiencing to some degree the end of the American evangelical church as we know it, we now have an opportunity to maintain a different vantage point as a church that shows up, stays put, and sees God's loving work in the world. When one follows the crucified Christ, it's inevitable that the character of love will go beyond sentiment. As R&B musician Musiq once sang, "Love, so many people use your name in vain." We can serve our world with a greater love than the reductionist, lesser symbols coopted by American idealism. Our vantage point, which is the vantage point of the cross and the resurrection, can train our sight with generosity and presence, our church spaces abiding in proximity to Christ's priorities.

Here's the shift and hope: by faith no church is meant to do this alone. We are not called to simply build churches, but to build churches that cultivate ecologies of grace. Sustained partnerships.

This does not render immediate results, but it is a generational work replete with signs of heaven in the here and now. We receive and interpret these signs and wonders in faith, knowing that "without faith it is impossible to please God" (Hebrews 11:6). Faith will nourish our imaginations in such a way that we begin to envision things once impossible as now inevitable, happening in ways only God can orchestrate.

What if we showed up for this call together?

ACKNOWLEDGMENTS

W RITING IS AN EXAMPLE of how God creates us as worlds reaching out, converging and collaborating with other worlds. I am grateful for Helen Lee at IVP for inviting me to enter the world of publishing, opening an avenue for our church journey to be shared with a larger audience. A special thanks as well to my editor, Anna Gissing, for your encouraging voice through each round of edits, fielding my many questions as a first-time author.

My discerning approach to walking in neighborhoods comes from my father, José Humphreys II, and my mother, Arcadia Humphreys. I am grateful for all of the walks we still take through the Lower East Side. My early thoughts about ministry in the city became further crystallized through my work with Richard Rivera, Pastor Marc Rivera, and Dr. Raymond Rivera. What a trio!

There were many other voices that informed the author of this book before it was conceived and throughout the writing process. *Gracias*, David Ramos and the Latinx Leadership Circle. Our theological reflection together and our endeavors to engage faith more courageously echo through my writing today. Thanks to Lisa Sharon Harper for providing me with more robust language to discuss God's very good gospel. I'm especially thankful to Keith Varnel Wallace, who was formative in embracing my African heritage these last twenty plus years. To Ruben Austria for opening my eyes to criminal justice and Julio Medina for welcoming me into the Exodus family, relationships that have driven me to reconcile the narrative gaps found in today's prison story.

I'm grateful for the many elders, friends, and pastors in the Evangelical Covenant Church family who have contributed to my formation as a person and pastor. To every person who participated in the life of Metro over this last decade, a special thanks. I'm grateful for those who would also respond to the radical invitation to life together at Hope House in East Harlem: Andy, Sonya, JJ, Chantilly, Nina, Jacob, Rachael, Tom, Melissa, Katie, Yudy, Alfredo, Hesed, Jared, Abigail, Mayra, and Javier.

NOTES

1 EL TESTIMONIO

15 *Perhaps we were, all of us*: James Baldwin, *The Fire Next Time* (New York: Vintage Books, 1963), 41.

18 *unraveling of shalom*: Cornelius Plantinga, *Not the Way It's Supposed to Be: A Breviary of Sin* (Grand Rapids: Eerdmans, 2010).

19 *In the Hebrew conception of the world*: Lisa Sharon Harper, *The Very Good Gospel: How Everything Wrong Can Be Made Right* (New York: Waterbrook, 2016), 31.

20 *dysfunctional transactions between people*: Charles Zastrow, *Introduction to Social Work and Social Welfare: Empowering People*, 10th ed. (Belmont, CA: Cengage Learning, 2010), 49.

21 *Stress hormones*: Shaili Jain, "Cortisol and PTSD, Part 1: An Interview with Dr. Rachel Yehuda," *Psychology Today*, June 15, 2016, www.psychologytoday.com/blog/the-aftermath-trauma /201606/cortisol-and-ptsd-part-1.

21 *children of certain Holocaust survivors*: Interview of Rachel Yehuda by Krista Tippet, "How Trauma and Resilience Cross Generations," *On Being*, July 30, 2015, https://onbeing.org /programs/rachel-yehuda-how-trauma-and-resilience-cross -generations.

24 *testimonio*: Eldin Villafane, *The Liberating Spirit: Toward an Hispanic American Pentecostal Social Ethic* (Grand Rapids: Eerdmans, 1993), 119.

2 THE "HERE I AMS" OF LIFE

31 *Come, follow me*: See Matthew 4:19; Luke 5:10.

38   *groups tend to be more sinful*: Reinhold Niebuhr, *Moral Man and Immoral Society* (New York: Macmillan Publishing Company, 1932).

42   *Paul's letter to the Galatians*: Galatians 2:11-19.

3 INCARNATIONAL

48   *who gets to tell the stories of bodies*: Brian Bantum helped me formulate this question through his award-winning article "Who Decides What My Body Means?" *Christian Century*, March 16, 2017, https://www.christiancentury.org/article /critical-essay/who-decides-what-my-body-means. I encountered a similar question in Dr. Bantum's book *The Death of Race*.

50   *It is still far easier*: Luis Pedraja, *Jesus Is My Uncle: Christology from a Hispanic Perspective* (Nashville: Abingdon Press, 1999), 73.

53   *we meet this Christ*: Orlando Costas, *Christ Outside the Gate: Mission Beyond Christendom* (Ossining, NY: Orbis Books, 1982).

      Mary Magdalene mistook Jesus for the gardener: Andy Crouch, *Playing God: Redeeming the Gift of Power* (Downers Grove, IL: InterVarsity Press, 2013), 78.

59   *Jesus preached the* basileia tou theou: M. Shawn Copeland, *Enfleshing Freedom: Body, Race and Being* (Minneapolis: Fortress Press, 2010), 57-58.

60   *The last will be first*: Matthew 20:16.

      Do not take the place of honor: Luke 14:8.

      Whoever is least in the kingdom: Matthew 11:11.

      Bring in the poor: Luke 14:21.

62   *this uneven discipline*: Lauren Camera, "Black Girls Are Twice as Likely to Be Suspended, in Every State," *U. S. News & World Report*, May 9, 2017, www.usnews.com/news/education-news /articles/2017-05-09/black-girls-are-twice-as-likely-to-be -suspended-in-every-state.

4 NAMING WHITENESS

66   *Los negros no tenían historia*: Elinor Des Verney Sinnette, *Arturo Schomburg: Black Bibliophile and Collector* (Detroit: Wayne State University Press, 1989), 13.

69   *across the cultural and racial spectrum*: For the purposes of this chapter I did not include the complexity of class, though this deserves further treatment for the church context.

71   *a facilitating reality*: Willie James Jennings, *The Christian Imagination: Theology and the Origins of Race* (New Haven, CT: Yale University Press, 2010), 275.

72   *this sense of always looking at one's self*: W. E. B. Du Bois, *The Soul of Black Folks* (New York: Dover Publications, 1994), 2.

73   *the diversity project in churches*: Korie Edwards, *The Elusive Dream: The Power of Race in Interracial Churches* (Oxford: Oxford University Press, 2008), 121.

78   *Christ is present in the world*: Reggie L. Williams, *Bonhoeffer's Black Jesus: Harlem Renaissance Theology and an Ethic of Resistance* (Waco, TX: Baylor University Press, 2014), 9.

5 STAYING PUBLIC

90   *church in jazz terms*: Peter Goodwin Heltzel, *Resurrection City: A Theology of Improvisation* (Grand Rapids: Eerdmans, 2012), 21.

96   *Shalom is what God declared*: Lisa Sharon Harper, *The Very Good Gospel: How Everything Wrong Can Be Made Right* (Colorado Springs: Waterbrook Press, 2016), back cover.

100   *An African proverb*: José Humphreys, "3 Ways to Cultivate Joy While Working for Change," Sojourners, www.sojo.net/articles /faith-action/3-ways-cultivate-joy-while-working-change. Used by permission.

101   *between Hope and Hades*: Gabriel Salguero, Metro Hope fifth-year anniversary sermon, February 2010, "The Church Located at the Corner of Hope and Hades."

6 REMAINING AT WORK

112   *the rule of the household*: Donald K. McKim, *Westminster Dictionary of Theological Terms* (Louisville, KY: Westminster John Knox Press, 1996), 270.

115 *The addition of small changes*: Adam Frank, "Could You Help Rewire Income Disparity?," NPR Cosmos and Culture, June 27, 2017, www.npr.org/sections/13.7/2017/06/27/534522821 /could-you-help-rewire-income-disparity.

cash mobs: This content originally appeared in José Humphreys, "Cash Mob Discipleship," *Covenant Companion*, July 15, 2015, http://covenantcompanion.com/2015/07/15/cash-mob -discipleship/.

7 STAYING TOGETHER

122 *Staying, we all know*: Jonathan Wilson-Hartgrove, *The Wisdom of Stability: Rooting Faith in a Mobile Culture* (Brewster, MA: Paraclete Press, 2010), 4.

126 *Imagine a people*: Willie James Jennings, *The Christian Imagination: Theology and the Origins of Race* (New Haven, CT: Yale University Press, 2010), 14.

134 *relationship of reciprocal concern*: Marcia Pally, *Covenant and Commonwealth: Theologies of Mutuality and Reciprocity* (Grand Rapids: Eerdmans, 2016), 155.

135 *trust, stability, compassion, and hope*: Tom Rath and Barry Conchie, *Strengths Based Leadership: Great Leaders, Teams, and Why People Follow* (New York: Gallup Press, 2008).

8 LOOK AGAIN

142 *In 2015 Barna conducted a study*: "New Research on the State of Discipleship," Barna Group, December 1, 2015, www.barna .com/research/new-research-on-the-state-of-discipleship.

Barna study: That being noted, Barna conducted a later study in 2016 on the differences in discipleship in black and white churches, where "black Christians are much more likely to believe that their personal spiritual lives have an impact on broader society (46% compared to 27% [of white Christians])."

143 *life's most persistent and urgent question*: Martin Luther King Jr., speech, Montgomery, Alabama, 1957.

146 *The number one abuse*: Jimmy Carter, "Why I Believe the Mistreatment of Women Is the Number One Human Rights

Abuse," TED talk, www.ted.com/talks/jimmy_carter_why_i
_believe_the_mistreatment_of_women_is_the_number
_one_human_rights_abuse.

146 *71 percent of trafficking victims*: Human Rights First, "Human
Trafficking by the Numbers," January 7, 2017, www.human
rightsfirst.org/resource/human-trafficking-numbers.

153 *The generous person*: Brad Young, *Jesus the Jewish Theologian*
(Grand Rapids: Baker Academic, 1995), 136.

9 CURATING HEAVEN

163 *Paul once wrote*: Philippians 3:10.

165 *A sacrament cannot be "rightly administered"*: Tom Faw Driver,
The Magic of Ritual (San Francisco: HarperSanFrancisco, 1991),
204.

10 *EL CULTO*

178 *sanctify the time*: Erica Brown, *Spiritual Boredom: Rediscovering
the Wonder of Judaism* (Woodstock: Jewish Lights Publishing,
2009).

180 *Ritual space "is not only"*: Nathan Mitchell, *Liturgy and the
Social Sciences* (Collegeville, MN: Liturgical Press, 1999), 75.

185 *compulsion to repeat the violence*: Serene Jones, *Trauma and
Grace: Theology in a Ruptured World* (Louisville, KY: Westminster John Knox, 2009), 29.

     the mind's meaning-making structures: Jones, *Trauma and
Grace*, 29.

     wanders and consistently replays: Jones, *Trauma and Grace*,
30.

188 *Oh, God, hear and answer us*: Michael Washington, "For Tonight's
Service of Lament," July 8, 2016, https://crossingintersections
.wordpress.com/2016/07/08/for-tonights-service-of-lament.

192 *James Cone describes how people had church in the Jim Crow
South*: James Cone, *The Cross and the Lynching Tree* (Maryknoll,
NY: Orbis Books, 2011).

193 *rituals of denial*: Paul Bradshaw and John Melloh, *Foundations
in Ritual Studies* (Grand Rapids: Baker Academic, 2007).

11 APOCALYPSE

197   *something apocalyptic written into the collective unconscious*: Edward F. Edinger, *Archetype of the Apocalypse: Divine Vengeance, Terrorism, and the End of the World* (Peru, IL: Open Court, 1999).

This way of writing: N. T. Wright, *Revelation for Everyone* (Louisville, KY: Westminster John Knox, 2011), 2.

198   *to stand out and stand apart*: Brian K. Blount, *Can I Get a Witness? Reading Revelation Through African American Culture* (Louisville, KY: Westminster John Knox, 2005), ix-x, 1.

199   *sacralizing of guns*: Warren J. Blumenfeld, "Christian Crusaders Urged to Arm for Liberty," *Huffington Post* blog, December 7, 2015, www.huffingtonpost.com/warren-j-blumenfeld/christian -crusaders-urged_b_8733876.html.

200   *"Love," in the early Christian sense*: Wright, *Revelation for Everyone*, 13.

201   *The great enemy of the church*: Stanley Hauerwas, *The Hauerwas Reader* (Durham, NC: Duke University Press, 2001), 526.

202   *I admit to being more in love*: Eugene Cho, *Overrated: Are We More in Love with the Idea of Changing the World Than Actually Changing the World?* (Colorado Springs: David C. Cook, 2014).

203   *It seems innocent enough*: Jonathan Aigner, "'Make America Great Again' Is Now a CCLI Licensed Christian Worship Song," *Ponder Anew*, July 2, 2017, www.patheos.com/blogs /ponderanew/2017/07/02/make-america-great-now-ccli -licensed-christian-worship-song.

206   *The political DNA of his church*: David Montero, "A Pastor in the Bible Belt Opened His Church to Refugees. Here's What Happened," *Los Angeles Times*, February 15, 2017, www.latimes .com/nation/la-na-evangelical-refugee-20170215-story.html.

207   *living with a refugee*: Montero, "A Pastor in the Bible Belt."

living above place: Paul Sparks, Tim Soerens, and Dwight Friesen, *The New Parish* (Downers Grove, IL: InterVarsity Press, 2014), 24.

210   *Your parish is a relational microcosm*: Sparks, Soerens, and Friesen, *New Parish*, 24.

C|C CHRISTIAN COMMUNITY
D|A DEVELOPMENT ASSOCIATION

The Christian Community Development Association (CCDA) is a network of Christians committed to engaging with people and communities in the process of transformation. For over twenty-five years, CCDA has aimed to inspire, train, and connect Christians who seek to bear witness to the Kingdom of God by reclaiming and restoring under-resourced communities. CCDA walks alongside local practitioners and partners as they live out Christian Community Development (CCD) by loving their neighbors.

CCDA Titles Available

Church Forsaken 978-0-8308-4555-2

Embrace 978-0-8308-4471-5

Making Neighborhoods Whole 978-0-8308-3756-4

The Next Worship 978-0-8308-4129-5

The Power of Proximity 978-0-8308-4390-9

Rethinking Incarceration 978-0-8308-4529-3

Seeing Jesus in East Harlem 978-0-8308-4149-3

Welcoming Justice 978-0-8308-3479-2

Where the Cross Meets the Street 978-0-8308-3691-8

White Awake 978-0-8308-4393-0